THE

HISPANIC AMERICANS

Also By Milton Meltzer

BOUND FOR THE RIO GRANDE:
THE MEXICAN STRUGGLE, 1845–1850

THE CHINESE AMERICANS

ALL TIMES, ALL PEOPLES:
A WORLD HISTORY OF SLAVERY

THE HUMAN RIGHTS BOOK

WORLD OF OUR FATHERS:
THE JEWS OF EASTERN EUROPE

TAKING ROOT:
JEWISH IMMIGRANTS IN AMERICA

NEVER TO FORGET:
THE JEWS OF THE HOLOCAUST

HUNTED LIKE A WOLF:
THE STORY OF THE SEMINOLE WAR

IN THEIR OWN WORDS:
A HISTORY OF THE AMERICAN NEGRO, 1619–1865

IN THEIR OWN WORDS:
A HISTORY OF THE AMERICAN NEGRO, 1865–1916

IN THEIR OWN WORDS:
A HISTORY OF THE AMERICAN NEGRO, 1916–1966

A PICTORIAL HISTORY OF BLACK AMERICANS
(WITH LANGSTON HUGHES AND C. ERIC LINCOLN)

LANGSTON HUGHES: A BIOGRAPHY

T H E
HISPANIC
AMERICANS

MILTON MELTZER

ILLUSTRATED WITH PHOTOGRAPHS BY
MORRIE CAMHI & CATHERINE NOREN

THOMAS Y. CROWELL • NEW YORK

Library of Congress Cataloging in Publication Data
Meltzer, Milton, 1915–
The Hispanic Americans.
Bibliography: p.
Includes index.
Summary: Discusses the social and economic problems
faced by twelve million Hispanic Americans who live and
work in the United States today.
1. Hispanic Americans—Juvenile literature.
[1. Hispanic Americans] I. Title. II. Series.
E184.S75M44   1982   973′.0468   81-43314
ISBN 0-690-04110-1   AACR2
ISBN 0-690-04111-X (lib. bdg.)

1 2 3 4 5 6 7 8 9 10
First Edition

Acknowledgments

We gratefully acknowledge permission to reprint material on the following pages: pp. 16–17, from "For Hispanos It's Still the Promised Land," by Paul and Rachel Cowan, copyright © 1975 by *The New York Times*; pp. 21–22, 89–90, from *Bernardo Vega's Memoirs*, a forthcoming publication from Monthly Review Press; pp. 20–21, "Unemployed," by Pedro Pietri, from his book of poems *Puerto Rican Obituary*, copyright © 1973 by Pedro Pietri, reprinted by permission of *Monthly Review Press*; pp. 44–47, from *First Generation*, by June Namias, copyright © 1978 by June Namias, reprinted by permission of Beacon Press; pp. 61–67, 102, from *Barrio Boy*, by Ernesto Galarza, copyright © 1971 University of Notre Dame Press; pp. 83–86, from an article by Grace Halsell in the July–August 1978 edition of *Agenda: A Journal of Hispanic Issues*, reprinted by permission of *Agenda*.

Contents

1	Escape to Life	1
2	First Settlers	7
3	In the Barrio	16
4	Island in the Sun	26
5	Family Portrait	37
6	From Havana to Miami	44
7	Ernesto's California	61
8	Across the Border	69
9	Pascual's Story	79
10	Pictures Can Lie	89
11	"We Will Not Lose What Is Ours"	100
12	Farm Workers on Strike	112
13	A Modern Slave Trade	117
14	Struggle for Justice	127
	Bibliography	141
	Index	145

People of Hispanic background or descent living in the United States come chiefly from the countries of the Americas—from Mexico, Cuba, and Puerto Rico, from Central and South America.

1

Escape to Life

There is a village high in the mountains of central Mexico that is without fathers or husbands for nine months of the year.

For those nine months, only women, children, and the old are to be found in the streets and houses.

The village is called Ahuacatlán, meaning "land of avocados." But the green fruit grows there no longer. Nor does anything else except a little corn and a few beans.

Where are the men?

A thousand of them, from their teens into their fifties, are in the United States.

Each autumn they go north, to labor as farmhands through the seasons until summer comes. Then Ahuacatlán knows a happy time. For in the summer the men return from the States with money and the gifts it can buy. Their wives and children eat better for a while. But then the money runs out, and the men are off again.

Year after year men like fifty-five-year-old Bernabé Garay go north from Ahuacatlán and hundreds of other villages in the blue-green Sierra Madre. They must migrate or starve. In the rural districts of this part of Mexico the harvests are so bad, and the people so poor and so sick, that crossing the border to the United States is an escape to life. Millions before Bernabé Garay took that route, and millions after him will do the same, unless the crushing poverty is somehow brought to an end.

As summer fades, Bernabé and his fellow villagers pile into a battered bus and travel for two days and nights to the Mexican border town of Sonoita. This is a jumping-off place for illegal entry into the United States. Early the next evening, José, the driver, arrives by arrangement with his truck and collects $600 from Bernabé and his friends to drive them to a desolate spot east of Sonoita where crossing the border is easy. The men simply pass through a gaping hole in the barbed wire fence and start walking north. They travel light in the desert night, killing snakes in the path, seeing no sign of the Border Patrol. At 9:30 P.M. they reach a pickup point off Arizona Highway 1. With the moon down and the sky pinpointed with innumerable stars, they wait for their next ride. Across the desert comes an old jalopy. At the wheel sits Ricardo, an eighteen-year-old smuggler of aliens. He collects $100 each from Bernabé and the six other men he will drive to Phoenix, and they speed off into the black night.

Dumped off at Phoenix, the men head for the citrus ranch where they worked the year before. At 8:00 the next morning they are all at work—hauling heavy canvas bags up and down the stepladders leaning against the tall lemon trees. By 5:30, Bernabé has filled his bag eighty-two times and has picked 3,690 pounds of lemons. He receives $41, a bit over a penny a pound. It is far more money than he could have earned in Mexico for a whole week's work— assuming he could have found a job there.

Not all of the Hispanic people who try to get jobs on the United States mainland come by the underground route. Some come legally—and Puerto Ricans, of course, are American citizens. A majority of migrant laborers are Mexicans, but some also come from South and Central America, and from the Caribbean Islands. Nor are all Hispanics looking for work on farms or ranches. Many seek jobs in industry or in the service trades.

But wherever they come from, however they enter the United States, they are driven by one force—hunger for work.

For the people of Mexico and the Caribbean, of Central and South America, the last decades have been a time of turbulent change. The gap between the rich and the poor nations of the world grows even wider. Many millions throughout Latin America know desperate hunger and poverty. No wonder so many people from the poor nations try to find a better life by moving to countries where they think they will have a better chance to live freely and decently.

The population explosion in the southern hemisphere is a major cause of migration. The number of workers looking for jobs has far outstripped the number of jobs to be found. It takes all the running people can do to stay in the same place. So, every year, thousands of Hispanic people enter other countries, by legal or illegal means. The United States is one of the places the migrants seek out.

Whatever the numbers leaving Latin America, they are but a small fraction of those who stay in their homelands. And of those who do come to the United States, about one out of three do not stay. They return home sooner or later.

Still, the Hispanic population of the United States is growing steadily. In the nation's largest city, New York, two million people—one out of every four—are of Hispanic birth or heritage.

In Los Angeles, a city founded by Mexicans, Hispanics now make up 28 percent of the population—they are the largest single ethnic group there. These 850,000 people (mostly Mexican) have helped to make Los Angeles second in size only to New York City.

Today, 40 percent of the people in Miami are of Spanish heritage. The city has 650,000 Hispanics; over 500,000 of them are Cuban. The experts say that within twenty years Los Angeles and Greater Miami will have populations that are over 50 percent Hispanic.

In Chicago, in Washington, D.C., in Kansas City, in Philadelphia, there are many thousands of Hispanics. It is not news that for a long time there have been large settlements of Hispanics in the Southwest. What *is* news is that in other parts of the country, sizable Hispanic communities have sprung up in the cities where there were no Hispanic people, or very few, only recently.

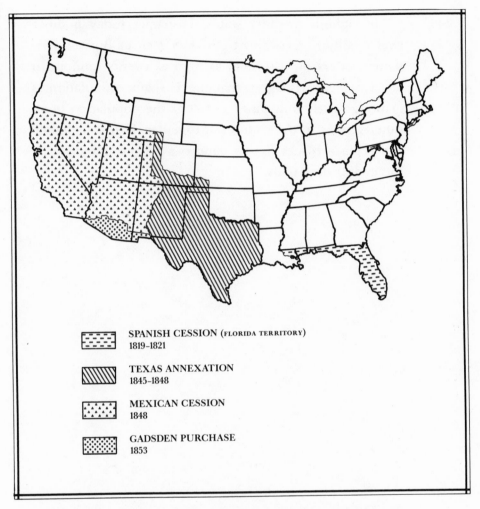

SPANISH CESSION (FLORIDA TERRITORY)
1819–1821

TEXAS ANNEXATION
1845–1848

MEXICAN CESSION
1848

GADSDEN PURCHASE
1853

This map shows those parts of the continental U.S. that were once Hispanic lands. In the southeastern corner is Florida Territory, ceded by Spain to the U.S. in 1819. West of the Mississippi is Texas, which was once Mexican, then became an independent republic, and was finally annexed by the U.S. in 1845. In the far west is the huge area—half of Mexico at the time—ceded to the U.S. in 1848 after Mexico's defeat in war; these lands are today the states of California, Utah, Nevada, and parts of Wyoming, Arizona, New Mexico and Colorado. The Gadsden Purchase area became part of the U.S. in 1853 under a treaty with Mexico.

Throughout the fifty states, Hispanics today number twelve million, according to the U.S. Census Bureau. Hispanic leaders put the total as high as twenty million. In any case, experts agree that the Hispanic population is growing nearly four times as fast as the population of all other groups in the nation put together. Hispanic people will replace blacks as the country's biggest minority by the end of the 1980s.

2

First Settlers

People call the Hispanic immigrants of today "newcomers."

We forget that Hispanics were the first Europeans to settle in what is now the United States. Decades before the English came, the Spaniards had planted colonies here.

The first Spaniards came on ships captained by Christopher Columbus. He was trying to find a new water route to the East by sailing westward. In the East he expected to gather gold, silver, spices, silks, perfumes, drugs, and converts to Christianity. When he touched Caribbean shores in 1492, he mistakenly thought he had landed on islands off the coast of Asia. He called the people who came out to greet him *los Indios,* or the Indians.

Columbus made four voyages across the Atlantic, and planted Spain's first permanent settlement in the New World. On the island of Hispaniola (now shared by the

Dominican Republic and Haiti) he built a fort; there he left men and supplies. The settlers hoped to get rich quickly by forcing the Indians to dredge for gold in the rivers. But there was not much gold, so the colonists took to farming and ranching. They raised cotton, sugarcane, and horses.

One Spaniard on Hispaniola, Juan Ponce de León, sailed from there to set up a colony on the island of Puerto Rico. While exploring islands near Puerto Rico, he came upon a long coastline. He thought it was a new island and named it Florida, claiming it for Spain in 1513.

A few years later, in 1526, Lucas Vásquez de Ayllón tried to found settlements on the coasts of North and South Carolina. Other Spaniards sailed down the East Coast from Nova Scotia to the Florida Keys and the Gulf Coast of Texas.

Thus much of the east coast of North America was mapped. But the land beyond the beaches was not explored until Núñez Cabeza de Vaca ventured inland. As his big expedition of soldiers, colonists, and priests struggled across rivers and through swamps and forests, they found no treasures. Many of de Vaca's men died, deserted him, or were captured and enslaved by the Indians. With only three other survivors, de Vaca wandered west and south until they came out on the Gulf of California in 1536, eight years after they had left Florida. On that shore they found another company of Spaniards who had sailed up the coast of Mexico.

These were not the first Spaniards to see the Pacific. Balboa had "discovered" it in 1513, the same year Ponce de León had "discovered" Florida. (I say "discovered" in quotation marks because of course the Indians—the Native Americans—had been there thousands of years before.)

Soon after de Vaca returned to Spain and reported on his travels, three Spanish expeditions set out to explore other parts of what is now the United States. One party sailed up the Gulf of California to the mouth of the Colorado River. Another crossed into New Mexico, and a third, led by Hernando de Soto, sailed from Cuba to Florida, where, in 1539, de Soto established a settlement at Tampa Bay. From there he ventured into Georgia and the Carolinas, Tennessee, and Alabama; crossed the Mississippi River; and went up the river into Arkansas, Missouri, and Oklahoma.

The next year, 1540, Francisco Vásquez de Coronado and his men explored the area that is now Arizona, New Mexico, and Texas, and then pushed on into Oklahoma and Kansas. By the summer of 1541, both de Soto and Coronado had reached the heartland of what would one day be the United States, their parties passing only a few hundred miles from each other.

The year their explorations ended—1542—another expedition from Mexico sailed up the west coast of Baja California, reached the site of San Diego, and then went north all the way to Oregon.

By 1600, Spain claimed lands her explorers had tracked across the North American continent from sea to sea, and she had planted a great many settlements in both North and South America. Among them was St. Augustine, Flor-

9

ida, the first permanent settlement made by Europeans in what is now the United States. Today hundreds of Spanish names pepper the American map.

For three hundred years, the Spanish controlled the land that is now the southern rim of the United States. Those huge holdings were Spain's until the middle of the nineteenth century.

Looking back now, it seems remarkable that so few men could take control of such an enormous part of the continent. What a lasting effect they have had! True, none of them found the treasures of gold and jewels they were hunting for. They could not know the America they wandered over was unimaginably rich in natural resources. One day the minerals, the oil, the forests, the soil would yield vast value to those who took advantage of them. Nor could the Spaniards guess that what they brought with them to the New World—the horses, cattle, sheep, goats, pigs, and poultry, the many fruits, the farming tools— would contribute hugely to the wealth of a nation yet to be born.

What have the Hispanic Americans of today in common with those Spanish conquerors and colonists of five hundred years ago? There is no direct "bloodline." There has been such an intermixture of peoples in the Americas that to speak of anyone's "pure blood" would be foolish.

Go back to the Spanish at the time of Columbus—their origins were very mixed, too. Any Spaniard was likely to be part Celt, part Phoenician, part Greek, part Roman, part Visigoth, part Arab, part African. All those people interbred at one time or another as history brought them together on the Iberian peninsula. And the Spaniards, already a savory mixture when they landed in the Americas, soon enriched their makeup with still other elements.

The early Spanish colonists and soldiers came without women. Out of the meeting of Spaniard and Indian came a new combination—children with Spanish fathers and Indian mothers. And then, the rise of the plantation system had its influence on the genetic mix. To turn a profit on sugar, tobacco, or cotton, a landowner had to produce on a large scale, using cheap labor. The Spanish settlers refused to do the hard work themselves, and turned to slave labor. They began with the Indians. When the Indians died quickly, the Spaniards imported African slaves, and interbred with them, too. Furthermore, the Indians and Africans, living in the same region, often intermarried.

In those parts of the Spanish Empire specifically linked to United States history, this mixture of peoples was the general rule. Only a few Spanish women ever entered the northern borderlands of the Empire. By the 1600s, a large part of the Spanish-speaking population of the New World was of mixed or non-European background.

Today, the Puerto Ricans—essentially the descendants of male Spanish immigrants who lived with Indian or African women—run almost the full range of color. As Puerto Ricans intermarry more and more with Anglo-Americans, they of course add Indian and African portions to the "Anglo" genetic mixture. Cubans and other Hispanic immigrants who marry Anglo-Americans also enrich our national stock. The Puerto Rican historian Arturo Morales Carrión says this about the special Hispanic blend:

11

We are people of all colors and hues. Ethnic mixture is our salient characteristic. A simple definition of the Hispanic could be: a person with a willingness to mix and therefore a person with a disposition to create new types of human relationships and new types of cultural forms, or to develop new perceptions of man and reality. Color to us is an accident, not a definition of the human person.

The Spanish language and culture is the common ground for Mexicans, Cubans, Puerto Ricans, and other Hispanics in the United States. Hispanic Americans differ from earlier waves of immigrants in two important ways. By and large, they remain physically close to their mother countries in Mexico and the Caribbean, in Central and South America. And they move back and forth between the United States and their homelands. This helps to keep their cultural traditions alive and strong. They do not have to dig into a remote past to find their roots. The influence of their heritage is felt in their everyday lives.

Although they have much in common, Hispanics differ in many ways too. To lump all Hispanics together and insist that they are exactly alike would be foolish. Each Hispanic group has its own identity, and each Hispanic person feels the importance of the differences between groups. A Puerto Rican does not like to be mistaken for a Cuban, just as someone from the South does not like to be called a Yankee.

Even in those things common to Hispanics there are meaningful differences. All Hispanics share the Spanish language, and most share the Catholic religion. But the Spanish language spoken today among Puerto Ricans differs from that spoken among Chicanos or Cubans. There are differences in words in the vocabulary, in pitch of the voice, in cadence of speech, in pattern of language. These differences have many sources: the regions people come from, the education they got, their political past, the way they make their living. . . .

The forms of Catholicism, too, differ from group to group. The religious practice of Hispanics from the Caribbean has been influenced by African traditions. In Central America, Indian traditions have had their effect. The role of the priesthood is shaped in part by a group's location—a rural priest's duties are somewhat different from an urban priest's.

Choosing up sides for a basketball game in Spanish Harlem, New York. (Catherine Noren)

Talks with Hispanics reveal how aware they are of their Hispanic character and how it differs from the Anglo character they meet in the United States. Hispanics see Anglos as too much concerned with material things. They themselves are more interested in human and spiritual values. Hispanics feel they are understanding and warm people, while Anglos are cold. Unlike most Anglos, Hispanics pay a great deal of attention to family unity, to personal warmth, to respect for their elders and respect for their own and other people's dignity. The Anglos, they say, judge people on the basis of color, not on what kind of person someone is. The Anglos cannot accept people of another color because they feel superior to them.

A Colombian put it this way: "They don't care for their fellow man, be it their father, son, or neighbor. They only care for *el numero uno*. Other people are not important."

A newcomer from Ecuador says, "The American ties himself too much to the law and forgets about help to his *prójimo* [fellow man]. A highly sophisticated style is part of the American style. We are more friendly and warm. They will continue a coldness despite an attempt to be warm. They create distances."

Of course, Hispanic people who have been here for some time cannot help but be influenced by the new life. Living in the United States inevitably brings changes in what they consider the Hispanic way of life.

"We have lost the custom of being sincere friends, of sharing with our neighbors," says one Hispanic.

"There are two sides to me," says another, "but I am still Dominican at heart. I have been here about twenty years, but I cannot forget where I came from."

A Puerto Rican woman born in the United States describes herself as "a Puerto Rican first and an American second. I feel we have been trying to become American for too long and we are forgetting our roots, our culture, and the values of our nationality."

3

In the Barrio

In a corner of Queens, a borough of New York City, there once lived a few hundred lonely Hispanics. Today, only twenty years later, there are well over 100,000 Hispanic Americans in this neighborhood, the Jackson Heights–Elmhurst–Corona area. This part of New York is now like a cosmopolitan Hispanic city. Colombians live in one section, Ecuadorians in a second, Dominicans in a third, and Puerto Ricans in a fourth. They have replaced the Italian, the Irish, and the Jewish people who used to live here but have moved up and out to the suburbs.

This is Roosevelt Avenue, the heart of the neighborhood:

The fast beat of a merengue *or a* cumbia *bouncing from a record store invites passersby to wiggle their hips and dance a few steps. A Hispanic is never far from the latest hometown ball scores or political events. All over Jackson Heights the newsstands are stacked with newspapers from Bogotá, Buenos Aires, Guayaquil, Santo Domingo, all of which arrive in New York a day or two after they are published. Nor is he far from his spiritual roots. There are Catholic and Pentecostal churches all over the neighborhood. Here and there are tiny shops whose windows are jammed with statues of saints, with paintings of the Blessed Virgin and Christ on the Cross. . . .*

The bodegas are owned by Dominicans, Cubans, and Argentinians. These industrious storekeepers work an average of 110 hours a week, and their wives and children often serve as cashiers and clerks. They stock the yucca and the yautia, the Goya rice and beans, the Bustelo coffee, the canned guavas and naranjillas that their customers have been raised to consider the heart of a satisfying meal. They also stock the special kitchen utensils their customers have always used: the espresso *coffee pots, the wooden* tostoneras *for flattening sliced green plantains, the* maté *pipes. They place trays of baked* dulces—*coconut squares, sweet guava-filled cakes— by the cash register to tempt their departing clients. Their prices are higher than those of nearby supermarkets. But the* bodeguero *performs an indispensable service—he speaks his customer's language, knows where to look for jobs, apartments, friendly doctors; he's part of the grapevine of gossip in Jackson Heights. And he extends credit.*

The Hispanics are proud of their barrio. Take Victor Maridueña, an Ecuadorian. His home in Jackson Heights is a popular center for his *paisanos* (fellow countrymen). His ham radio set picks up the *fútbol* (soccer) games in Guayaquil and Quito, and he relays the scores to friends who call from all over New York.

Maridueña says, "We've revitalized this neighborhood. You don't see any abandoned housing here—you see buildings going up. No stores are empty—new businesses are opening all the time."

At La Marqueta, a covered market that runs for five blocks beneath the Park Avenue railroad tracks in East Harlem. Merchants sell meat, fish, produce, clothes, recordings, houseware, jewelry, and a hundred other things. (Catherine Noren)

Across the East River, in Manhattan, are the streets of Spanish Harlem. This is one of New York's many Puerto Rican neighborhoods. Of the two million Hispanics in New York, over half are Puerto Ricans. Here old tenements block out the sun and concrete covers the land. The tropics are only a memory. In winter the children warm themselves at bonfires built on vacant lots. When summer comes, the kids play on the same lots, which are covered with rubble and garbage and broken glass and empty beer cans. They twist open a fire hydrant and dance and yell in the arc of silver water shooting across the street. In Spanish Harlem, a much older Hispanic community, the people live poorly.

The old and the new in Spanish Harlem: abandoned tenements next to new housing projects. (Catherine Noren)

For most Hispanics, wherever they may live, it is hard to find jobs that pay well. And for many, it is hard to find any job at all. Automation has meant the death of many kinds of jobs once opened to unskilled immigrants. Pedro Pietri, a poet born in Ponce, Puerto Rico, worked on and off for years in various jobs, all of them menial. He tells what it is like to be

UNEMPLOYED

he gets on the train
at 125th street
and st nickalaus avenue
white shirt black tie
gray suit shoes shine
new york times help
wanted ads under his arm
his hair is neatly
process his wristwatch
does not function
the diamondless ring
he wears cost five dollars
on the block after
all the stores
close down for the day
on the train he takes
out his wallet & counts
500 imaginary dollars
after 59th street
came 42nd street & 8th avenue
& he gets out the train
& walks to the nearest
vending machine
& deposits a nickel

for a pack of dentine
& stares into the broken mirror
of the vending machine
for the next fifteen minutes
assuring himself
that he is looking good
and then he proceeds
to the employment
agencies and five
hours and three
hot dogs and two
hamburgers one pack
of cigarettes and
one pint of wine later
he is still jobless

The jobs most Puerto Ricans find on the mainland are the lowest paid and the hardest. These people start at the bottom of the ladder, doing manual labor. There are so many of them in the hotel and restaurant trades that those businesses would be helpless without them. Puerto Rican women are a big part of the work force in the garment industry.

Back in the early 1900s, it was New York's cigar factories that gave work to most Puerto Rican immigrants. One of those *tabaqueros* was young Bernardo Vega. His workplace, like most others, had an official "reader" who read aloud in Spanish from novels or history or political works. The books were chosen by vote of the workers; each *tabaquero* paid twenty-five cents a week to support the reader. No one ever fell asleep on the job. You earned and learned at the same time. Vega recalls:

During the readings at "El Morito" and other factories, silence reigned supreme—it was almost like being in church. [But] whenever we got excited about a certain passage we showed our appreciation by tapping our cotters on the workbenches.

At the end of each session there would be discussion of what had been read. Conversation went from one table to another without any interruption of our work. Though nobody was formally leading the discussion, everyone took turns speaking. . . . Should dates or questions of fact provoke discussion, there was always someone who insisted on going to the "donkey-slayers" (mataburros). . . . *That's what we called reference books. It was not uncommon for one of the workers to have an encyclopedia right there on his workbench.*

I remember times when a tabaquero *would get so worked up defending his position in a polemic that he didn't mind losing an hour's work—it was piecework—and trying to prove his point. He would quote from the books at hand, and if there weren't any in the shop he'd come back the next day with books from home, or from the public library.*

In about 1940, Puerto Ricans began coming to the mainland to do farm work. Migrant workers have always been treated badly; the Puerto Ricans were no exception. The Puerto Rican Department of Labor tried to improve conditions. Mainland employers coming to the island to recruit farm labor had to sign contracts guaranteeing minimum pay, and setting out working and living conditions. From then on, about 20,000 contract farm workers came up to the mainland each year. And as many as 70,000 a year came without contracts. They harvested tobacco, potatoes, sugar beets, vegetables, and fruit, working in many states. Often the laborers would decide to stay on the mainland, settling in towns near their places of work. When relatives and friends joined them, the Hispanic communities grew.

The contracts did not ensure eternal peace. Puerto Rican seasonal farm workers have struck more than once for higher wages and better conditions. They say they would rather organize and bargain for themselves than rely on the contracts employers have made with the island's labor department.

The farm workers have much to complain about. Their pay is often less than half that of factory workers. They receive no overtime pay, although they work up to seventy hours a week to get the crops in. There are farm labor camps with no hot water, no food, no electricity. The camps are overcrowded, have leaky bathrooms, have no screens; garbage is not picked up, and the camps attract rats, flies, and bedbugs. Some farms fail to provide water and portable toilets in the fields. As we will see in Chapter 8, another group of Hispanic farm workers, the Mexicans, have been treated just as badly.

Farm laborers are not the only ones who have it bad. Over the years, a number of Puerto Ricans have climbed the ladder to more skilled work and higher pay. But still, surveys show that in New York City, for example, two out of five Puerto Rican families live in poverty.

When Puerto Rican men advance, it is usually to become craftsmen and skilled workers. Both men and women may find white-collar jobs as clerks or salespeople. Some gain higher training and enter professional and technical fields.

A small business class has grown up in the neighborhoods where many Hispanics live. In the 1970s, there were 10,000 businesses and banks owned by Hispanics in New York City. The barrios are dotted with small stores that have been opened by hardworking immigrants who saved a little money. Often the owners of such stores are as poor as the people they serve. One-half of the bodegas are small food stores. The others are retail and service businesses: beauty parlors, barbershops, laundries, drugstores, record stores, jewelry stores. They are usually family owned, and have to compete with chain stores and department stores. No wonder many of them are small, poor, and shaky.

Bilingual signs in the Washington Heights neighborhood of New York show what a large Hispanic community the stores serve. (Catherine Noren)

Dreams become reality in ArtsConnection's three-year scholarship program, where a trampoline is training ground for future high fliers at New York's Big Apple Circus. Many of the students who participate in the program are Hispanic Americans. (Catherine Noren)

How do Hispanics see their position today? To find out, a team of reporters from the *New York Times* recently interviewed nearly six hundred Hispanic New Yorkers, the majority of them Puerto Ricans. Half said they are better off than their parents. One in four think they are in the same position as their parents. And the others believe they are worse off.

Today, about two million Puerto Ricans live on the mainland. If so many think they are badly off, why did they come? And why don't they go back? A look at life in Puerto Rico may give the answer.

4

Island in the Sun

The green, mountain-ribbed island of Puerto Rico is at the eastern end of the Caribbean Sea, a thousand miles from Florida. It is only one hundred miles long and thirty-five miles wide—about the size of Connecticut. After Ponce de León planted a colony there, Spain made the island a military fortress to protect the sea route to her other colonies. Puerto Rico remained a Spanish colony for nearly four hundred years.

It was in the 1800s that the Puerto Ricans began to feel they were a nation. Although most of the native people of the island had been killed off, the Spanish settlers, as we saw before, had intermarried with the survivors, and later with African slaves. The three peoples blended together in time; they became one people, with one culture, and this was the new Puerto Rican nation.

Agriculture was the island's way of life. At first, small

independent farmers lived on what they grew. But then a few planters got control of very large estates, and they began to produce cash crops, especially sugar. They used slaves or hired farm workers, and paid so little that many of the islanders lived in great poverty. There were several slave revolts. In 1873 slavery was abolished. Although slaves were a small minority on the island, the African culture has had a strong influence on diet, language, music, and religion in Puerto Rico.

The desire for independence grew among the islanders as the power of the Spanish Empire decreased. Spain tried to keep the colony on a tight rein, to control its trade and make sure of tax collection. The Puerto Ricans resented this—and the whites born on the island resented it most. These native-born whites were called *criollos,* or Creoles. They disliked the whites from the parent country, who looked down upon them and took the best positions in government for themselves. The Creoles—who far outnumbered Spanish whites—could get rich through landholding or trade. But they wanted political control, too.

When the Creoles found ways to get around restrictive Spanish laws, Spain offered reforms to keep things peaceful. But the Puerto Ricans were not satisfied, and tried to loosen the reins still more. Secret revolutionary societies formed on the island, as they did elsewhere throughout Spain's colonies.

By 1825, nothing of the Spanish Empire in the New World remained but the islands of Puerto Rico and Cuba. One after another the colonial peoples of Latin America had won their freedom from Spain.

In 1868 there was a short-lived uprising in Puerto Rico, led by Ramon Emeterio Betances. Leaders of the independence movement marched into the small town of Lares and proclaimed the Republic of Puerto Rico. But the revolt was quickly put down, as was another in 1897.

The United States had long been interested in Puerto Rico and Cuba. American companies owned sugar plantations and other businesses in the islands. Political and military leaders in the United States had often talked openly of the need to expand beyond the nation's continental borders. They wanted to spread American power across the whole North American continent. That spirit had led to war with Mexico in the 1840s.

In 1898, the sinking of the battleship *Maine* in Havana harbor, which the U.S. blamed on Spain, gave American war hawks the excuse they needed to declare war. American military forces seized the Philippines (a Spanish colony), Puerto Rico, and Cuba. The six-week Spanish-American War ended in Spain's defeat. The United States took possession of Puerto Rico and the Philippines, and also got control of Cuba.

Over the next fifty years, Congress passed various laws granting a degree of civilian rule to Puerto Rico. But basic control remained in the hands of the President and Congress. In 1917, Puerto Ricans were given U.S. citizenship (they weren't asked if they wanted it), and in 1947 they were given the right to elect their own governor. Puerto Rico, for so long a Spanish colony, was still a colony, if now under the American flag.

Not content with taking over the government, the United

States tried to "Americanize" Puerto Rico's culture. English was made the official language for schools and government, even though most Puerto Ricans spoke only Spanish. President Theodore Roosevelt said the United States had the superior culture, and that the Puerto Ricans must adopt it. It was not until 1945 that Spanish was reestablished as the basic language in the schools. English was required as a second language.

After the United States took over, the island's economic life changed rapidly. Heavy taxes on property and tight credit bankrupted not only the estate owners but the small farmers as well. They had to sell their holdings, and most of the land went to American sugar corporations. The result was the end of diversified farming. Thousands of small farmers, having lost their land, became low-paid workers in the cane fields and sugar mills. Sugar became king. And sugar was the island's curse. Puerto Rico was locked into a one-crop economy. What the people produced was not consumed by them, but was sold abroad to profit outsiders. And what they consumed was not produced by them, but was brought in from outside. The pattern was set: outside control of everything important.

For the farm workers, raising sugar was like a sentence of death. Work lasted only a few months a year. In the spring the workers planted the cane, and in the winter they harvested it. The rest of the year they had no work, and starved. If they did not die of hunger, malnutrition led to hookworm, malaria, tuberculosis. They lived in shacks of wood and straw, with bare earthen floors and no furniture. There was no welfare; the only "social security" was the tradition of *jíbaros* (poor country people) always helping one another. Tens of thousands were put out of work altogether as machines replaced farm labor. There was no birth control. The slums kept growing. They spread like a fungus over San Juan and other cities as hungry people left the hills for the towns.

Puerto Rico was soon being called "the poorhouse of the Caribbean." People trying to change that label formed a new political party, the Popular Democrats. This party, led by Luis Muñoz Marín, won control of the island legislature in 1940. Then World War II broke out; the United States poured many millions of dollars into building military bases and roads on the island, and took jobless youth into the armed forces. With the island treasury fattened, Muñoz Marín began land reform and a rural housing program.

After the war, Muñoz Marín launched a new economic plan called "Operation Bootstrap." The goal was to raise living standards by attracting industry and placing factories where there were many jobless people. Not the farm, but the factory, would be the key to Puerto Rico's economic future. It was arranged that American investors would not have to pay taxes to Puerto Rico or to the United States. The fact that they could pay lower wages on the island than on the mainland also encouraged Americans to open factories in Puerto Rico.

For twenty-five years, the plan seemed to work. By 1975, some 1,700 new factories—making chemicals, textiles, electrical instruments—had set up shop on the island. Over 140,000 new jobs in industry had been created. The con-

struction industry boomed, and so did the tourist trade.
The number of farm workers in those years dropped from
one out of three employed Puerto Ricans to one out of
twenty.

The island had turned into an urban society. Life expec-
tancy reached seventy-two years, and almost everyone had
learned to read and write. The annual per capita income
rose from $278 in 1948 to $1,865 in 1974.

This was a big improvement, and compared to living
standards in the rest of Latin America, Puerto Rico now
was doing well. But Puerto Rico had been under U.S. control for over seventy years. How well was the island doing
compared to the fifty states? In 1940, Puerto Rico's per
capita income was 80 percent less than the per capita income in Mississippi, the poorest state. In 1970—thirty
years later—Puerto Rico's per capita income was still that
much lower than Mississippi's (and Mississippi was still
the poorest state). While pay had gone up, prices had gone
still higher.

Many problems with Operation Bootstrap began to show
up in the 1970s. The factories all needed sewage systems,
electricity, water. Since the factories were tax free, the
Puerto Ricans had to pay taxes to foot the big bills. Industries using a large amount of labor found they could pay
even lower wages in other countries. They closed their
factories in Puerto Rico and moved abroad. No new factories were built, and there was a construction slump. Both
construction and factory workers lost jobs. Tourism slowed
down as rich Americans hunted for new pleasure spots.
When times got bad on the mainland, middle-class Ameri-

cans stayed at home. The Puerto Ricans' taxes went up; at the same time, the island's budget was slashed, and the pay of government workers was frozen.

When food stamps were introduced on the island in the 1970s, about 60 percent of the people proved eligible. Puerto Rico became more and more dependent upon federal welfare money. Unemployment grew rapidly. The official figure showed 18 percent unemployment in 1980— high enough!—but some economists said it was really nearer 40 percent, a figure never reached on the mainland even during the Great Depression.

Even during the period when Puerto Rico was considered an "economic miracle," it was emigration that had made things look better than they were. Between 1945 and 1970 about one-third of Puerto Rico's people had left to seek a new life on the mainland. That huge outflow helped to lower unemployment back home.

Migration to the mainland was nothing new. Puerto Ricans had lived in the United States since the early 1800s. Still, only a very small number came at first. The trickle increased after Puerto Ricans were made U.S. citizens in 1917. Then thousands began to move. Now they were not immigrants, but migrants, and it was easier to make the change. Within a few years, Puerto Ricans had settled in almost every state, though most chose New York.

Throughout the 1920s and 1930s they came, to learn a trade, make some money, and then go back home to Puerto Rico. By 1940 there were 60,000 Puerto Ricans living in New York City. The stream of migrants became a torrent in the years after World War II. Over 40,000 islanders came each year, year after year. Then, as now, jobs were scarce on the island. And the population was growing quickly—not because of any rise in the birthrate (in fact, the birthrate had been dropping), but because of improved public health, which meant more Puerto Ricans were living longer. With the U.S. economy booming, mainland employers sent down to the island for workers to fill jobs in the garment industry and in the growing "service" field—hotel and restaurant work and housecleaning. As plane fares dropped, Puerto Ricans found it easier to fly north. Politicians on the island encouraged migration. It was a "safety valve." It reduced pressure for jobs at home and helped keep things quiet. It seemed an easy way out.

Has migration proved to be the answer to Puerto Rico's basic problems? The story of Angel and Aurea Ortiz shows that it has not. They are just one Puerto Rican couple living on the mainland. But what has happened to them will tell us a lot.

Angel and Aurea Ortiz live in Hoboken, New Jersey. He is nearing forty, she's six years younger. Hoboken, a small city across the Hudson River from New York, has many garment factories, which has drawn 10,000 Puerto Ricans to live there. Angel works as a coat presser in one of them, and Aurea as a seamstress in another.

With their four children, they live in a four-room apartment in a mixed neighborhood—Irish, Italian, black, as well as Puerto Rican. Their rent is not too high, and together they make about $450 a week before taxes. They have an old car, a TV set, and a savings account.

Hispanics are a considerable part of the labor force throughout the garment industry. In this unionized undergarment shop, four out of five workers are Hispanic. (Catherine Noren)

Migration has shaped the lives of the Ortizes and their families. Angel's father had come alone to the mainland a dozen times to do seasonal farm labor, then return to his family with his savings. His three sons all followed him. Angel came here at sixteen, worked as a dishwasher in Massachusetts, and at twenty became an apprentice in the garment trade in Hoboken, where his two brothers had jobs.

Aurea's parents came up in 1949, when she was a baby, settling in the Bronx, the northernmost borough of New York City. Both parents worked in a belt factory, and ran a grocery store on the side. They dreamed of returning to Puerto Rico to stay. Once they went back and opened a grocery store, but it failed, and they returned to New York.

On several lines of the New York subway system, Spanish signs and advertisements are as common as English. (Catherine Noren)

Aurea dropped out of school at fifteen to work in a coat factory in Hoboken. She met Angel on the job, and they got married.

Angel and Aurea have done pretty well here, compared with other Puerto Ricans, but still they feel a strong emotional tie to the island and its culture. And, of course, they have family and friends there. Angel wanted their children to be brought up in Puerto Rico so they would know who they are and where they come from. That's why the Ortizes speak Spanish at home—to make sure their children learn the mother tongue.

In 1972 the Ortizes heard business was getting better and more jobs were available in Puerto Rico. So they sold their belongings and flew down with their children. But while there were some jobs, they were not *good* jobs. Angel and Aurea could find nothing to compare in pay or position with what they had had in the States. Two years later, with their savings and unemployment compensation gone, they returned to their old jobs in Hoboken.

A year later, they tried it again. With family help they built a house in Guayama, near where Angel's father had retired to live on Social Security. The job situation was no better. Aurea worked in a panty hose factory, but her pay was a third less than her Hoboken earnings. Angel commuted by car to a fish cannery in Ponce, but there, too, wages were low, and he said, "You couldn't even talk union." Besides, he said, "The Puerto Rican who came from the States was looked at with suspicion." Angel quit and bought a food concession outside a factory in Guayama. But his and Aurea's income together was barely half what they had earned on the mainland.

In 1977, they boarded up their house and again got their old jobs back, in Hoboken.

The Ortizes still plan to return to their homeland. But not for factory jobs—they are all poor jobs. Next time Angel wants to open an auto parts shop, after learning the business in night school.

Puerto Rican working-class families face hard choices. Life in the mainland cities gets worse and worse—buildings burned out, neighborhoods rotting, schools failing to do their job, inflation slashing the dollar, unemployment rising. The Ortizes are always drawn back to the familiar life on the island. But that culture, too, they feel, is fast disappearing.

What to do?

5

Family Portrait

Immigrants are coming into the United States from almost every country, territory, and island of the globe. They shape a nation far more diverse in race, language, and ethnicity than it was a hundred years ago when immigrants from southern and eastern Europe began pouring through Ellis Island. Today a fourth of New York's population is of Hispanic birth or heritage. Not long ago most of them were Puerto Ricans. But now greatly increasing numbers from other Latin countries are arriving, especially from the Dominican Republic, Colombia, Ecuador, and Cuba.

The Dominicans are rapidly replacing Puerto Ricans as the major Hispanic group in some parts of New York. It was estimated that by 1980 there were already some 300,000 to 500,000 Dominicans in New York.

Paul and Fanfi Vinas emigrated from the Dominican Republic in the 1970s. On their Caribbean island nation of

The Vinas family keeps in touch with home through Paul's mother, Bertha (center), who is on a four-month visit from the Dominican Republic.

6 million people, a fourth of the population is unemployed and another fourth is underemployed. Dictators, coups, and violence—mixed with such natural disasters as epidemics, hurricanes, and tropical storms—left little hope for a life of peace and comfort. In New York Paul is superintendent of a large apartment building in Washington Heights, a fast-growing Dominican community. He and Fanfi have two children, Paul Jr. and Marlene, with a third on the way. Ambitious for their family to move ahead, Paul adds to his income by cleaning bank lobbies on weekends and studying electronics at night school.

(Photographs in this chapter by Catherine Noren)

Fanfi Vinas with her children in front of their apartment building.

Paul tends to a boiler in the apartment house where he is a superintendent. The family has a two-bedroom apartment in the basement.

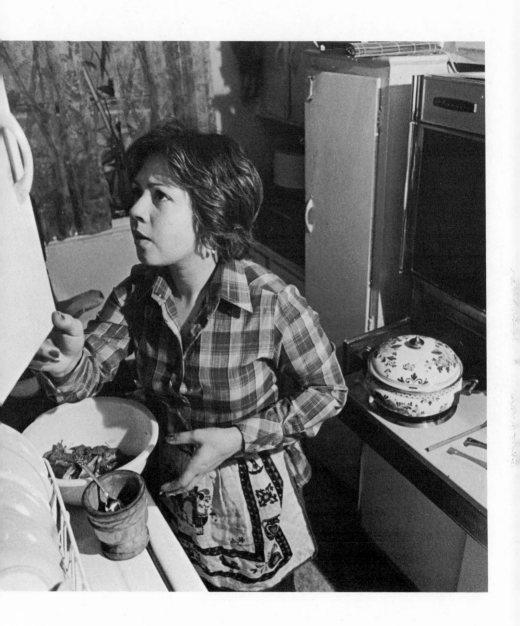

Fanfi prepares dinner for the family.

Paul sweeps the lobby of a downtown Citibank while his daughter watches.

(Facing page) Paul Jr., in the first grade at P.S. 189, works on a lesson. Either Paul or Fanfi picks him up every day to walk him home from school.

6

From Havana to Miami

In August or July we got a telegram in the middle of the night saying that we were authorized to go. I remember being excited at first, then I really felt bad. I remember crying. I remember looking back. I said to myself, "This is the last time you're going to look back." I remember I kept on looking back at my house and feeling very bad, very sad, and then going to Havana and going to the plane. . . .

That was eleven-year-old Rodolfo de León, a Cuban boy from the rural province of Camagüey. In 1962, with his mother and brother, he left his homeland for Miami. His father's business had been taken away by Fidel Castro's revolutionary government. The family decided to leave, as many thousands of Cubans did. Rodolfo's father stayed behind for a while to take care of family matters.

In Miami, the United States government gave Rodolfo's
mother $100 a month to get them started. It was hard
to find a cheap place to live, but at last they got one:

*We were renting the apartment for $72, and so we had $28
for the month. That meant a dollar a day. We lived on that for
I think about a year and a half. Aside from my mother baby-
sitting for about $2 for six hours, that was the only income we
had.*

*I remember in that place we had only one pillow. One day my
brother and I started fighting for the pillow. I started chasing him.
My mother was chasing us. Then my mother broke down crying.
We stopped. I felt really bad.*

*And we were eating bad food. It was not only bad, but we
were eating it constantly. Canned government meat. A whole year.
Breakfast. Lunch. Dinner. And beans. My mother would soak them
overnight, and she would spend the whole next day cooking. We
had this pot that we found. . . .*

When school opened, Rodolfo was put in the fourth
grade. In Cuba he had been in the eighth. He felt odd,
much bigger and older than the others in his class. He
would bring his Spam meat sandwiches for lunch. They
smelled, and the other kids would move away from him.

The boys tried to find ways to make money, to help
out their mother:

*My brother heard of this place where you could pick up doughnuts
and sell them—make a couple of dollars. The first day they left
us the doughnuts and a metal case to carry them in. We went
out with this stuff and walked around. Finally we found this guy
out mowing his lawn. He called us over. He said he wanted one.*

We gave him the bag. As he gave us the money he must have realized we were Cubans, not American kids. He took the package he'd bought and threw it in the garbage.

My brother was really upset. He was really hurt. I wasn't so much hurt but I figured—what were we going to do with all those doughnuts? Later on my mother wound up paying for the rest of the doughnuts. We didn't try to sell the rest. My mother had to pay $6 for them. We ate stale doughnuts for weeks.

It was hard for Rodolfo to watch his mother worrying all the time:

She was trying to get work. I remember she finally found work before my father came, for maybe four, five, or six months. She was working in a camarónera, *shrimp packing. Her fingers, a piece of her hand is wasted, you can see it. It's from peeling shrimps. She probably came home with $30 after about forty, forty-five hours. She came home at five, maybe six o'clock.*

Rodolfo grew more and more anxious to see his father again. But politics kept making it impossible for the father to leave Cuba. Finally, he was allowed out, and reached Miami by boat:

It was very hard, the first time I saw him. He looked very different, and I just didn't react the way I used to. And ever since then I haven't reacted the same way. Before we left Cuba, it was more like Daddy, Daddy—you know, father. It was more he represented something else before, and now he didn't. Something had been taken away. He didn't have the power he had before, the image I had of him.

My father couldn't work, couldn't find work. When he did, he found it in Boca Raton, sixty miles away from Miami. He picked tomatoes. They had a car pool, and some guy took him. So he

had to pay, I don't know how much. He went at about five o'clock
in the morning and came back at about ten o'clock at night. He
got paid $6 a day. . . .

Rodolfo de León is but one of half a million Cuban
refugees who have come to Miami. He did not stay there.
Eventually he left for Boston, where he took a college
degree in economics. Some years ago he became an American citizen.

Like Rodolfo, thousands of other Cubans have settled
in many other parts of the country, including New York
and New Jersey. New York City's Cuban population of
110,000 makes it the second largest Cuban-American community. Miami, of course, is the largest.

The Cubans are different from any other group that
has emigrated to the United States. First, the majority of
them are political refugees. Most other immigrants come
seeking work and a decent standard of living. The political
refugee's main goal is to settle where he can be free. In
the case of the Cubans, they migrated so they could live
in a democratic society with a private enterprise system.

Second, most of the Cubans come from the upper levels
of Cuban society. The majority are professionals, or skilled
or white-collar workers. Two out of five have some college
education. And most of them had yearly incomes above
the average in Cuba.

But they fled their homes because they did not like the
changes Fidel Castro began to make in Cuba after he led
the overthrow of Batista.

Cuba, like Puerto Rico, was discovered by Columbus

About 100,000 Cubans live in Hudson County, New Jersey, across the river from New York. The newcomers have made Union City one of the biggest "Little Havanas" outside Miami. Mostly working class, they seek jobs in small industries or offer services of their own. Here, Cuban enterprise dominates a Union City neighborhood. (Catherine Noren)

nearly five hundred years ago. It is the largest island in the West Indies. Shaped like a fish leaping out of the sea, the island is 730 miles in length and averages 50 miles in width. Its area is about the size of Pennsylvania.

The Spanish settlers soon established several towns in Cuba, including Havana. Just as in Puerto Rico, the Spaniards forced the Indians to mine for gold. When the Indians revolted, African slaves were brought in.

Because white settlers did not come to Cuba in large numbers for more than two hundred years, blacks became central to the island's life. Whether slave or free, blacks worked the goldfields, mined and smelted copper, herded cattle on the ranches, raised food on small farms. In the towns, they handled every kind of job. Even in the 1800s, when mass migration of whites from Spain began, Cuba's blacks held on to the jobs requiring special skills.

Sugar became king on this Caribbean island, too. Huge estates were worked by slaves or by free blacks; this system had the same blighting effect in Cuba as it had in Puerto Rico. White planters and businessmen ignored the needs of the mass of Cubans. They were happy with a one-crop economy, and abundant cheap labor meant they got very high profits.

The wealthy *criollos* in Cuba disliked being ruled from Spain. But they feared that a struggle for independence would lead to a black uprising. They preferred a Spanish colony to a black republic such as Haiti had become. So Cuba, like Puerto Rico, remained a Spanish colony long after the rest of the Spanish Empire had melted away.

As colonial rule became more and more corrupt, some

Cubans did try to rebel against it. The most famous rebel was the poet and journalist José Martí. Driven into exile at the age of sixteen, he raised funds abroad and gathered arms. In 1895, he and his followers landed near Santiago de Cuba. Martí was killed in a battle with the Spaniards soon after. His followers went into the Sierra Maestra mountains and launched guerrilla raids from there.

The attempts of the Cuban patriots to gain freedom won sympathy from many Americans. Business leaders and politicians, however, wanted to get control of the island for themselves. They saw it as a good place for investments and military bases.

When the United States defeated Spain in the war of 1898, the Spaniards cleared out of Cuba and Puerto Rico. From 1898 to 1902, Cuba was occupied by American military forces; meanwhile Puerto Rico, as we have seen, became a U.S. possession. The United States said it had invaded Cuba in 1898 to secure its independence from Spain. But American leaders wanted to ensure that Cuba would be a safe and agreeable neighbor. In 1902 Cuba became a republic, but because of the Platt Amendment its status was really more that of an American colony. Passed by the U.S. Congress in 1901, the Platt Amendment gave the United States the right to install naval stations on the island, and to mobilize its military forces in Cuba whenever there was danger to "life, property, and individual freedom," or if Cuban independence should be threatened. Cuba was required to make the terms of the Amendment part of its new constitution. The Platt Amendment remained in force until 1934, and it allowed the U.S. Marine Corps to intervene in Cuban affairs many times.

Americans made big investments in Cuba. Soon much of the island's best land was under American control. Both business and government became corrupt under what were, after all, colonial conditions. If sugar had dominated the economy before, to the detriment of the workers, now things were even worse. Sugar brought fat profits to American corporations, but only poverty to Cuban workers.

Cuban students and intellectuals began to work for reform. In the late 1940s, Fidel Castro, who had taken a law degree at Havana University, became the leader of a political party in Havana that was opposed to the Cuban dictator, Fulgencio Batista y Zaldívar (called Batista). Batista had been in control since 1933. In 1956 Castro made the Sierra Maestra mountains the base for a guerrilla war against Batista. Within three years Castro and his followers had overthrown Batista's government.

The revolutionaries believed Cuba could not be truly free so long as the United States controlled so much of the economy. Since Cuban business was closely tied to American business, Castro felt the system of private enterprise had to be ended. Furthermore, he said, only a socialist system could guarantee the people's freedom and a decent standard of living. By the end of 1960, Castro's revolutionary government was in control of all of Cuba's resources—land, industry, and commerce. With their profitable Cuban holdings taken away, American businessmen were very upset.

Because Cuba was not self-sufficient, Castro tried to develop trade with the United States, but was turned down by the federal government. Forced to seek aid elsewhere, Castro turned to the Communist-bloc countries for sup-

A Cuban grocery and butcher shop in Union City, New Jersey. (Catherine Noren)

plies, technical assistance, and military equipment. The United States called for a worldwide embargo on trade with Cuba. While some countries continued to trade with her, the embargo placed a heavy burden on Cuba.

As the connection between Cuba and the Soviet Union became ever closer, the United States broke diplomatic relations with Cuba and made plans to overthrow Castro. American government agencies organized, trained, and equipped an invasion force of anti-Castro Cuban exiles in Central America. In 1961 these men landed on Cuban shores, but were swiftly killed or captured by Castro's troops. This was the famous Bay of Pigs invasion. The defeat was very embarrassing to the United States. The next year, the Soviet Union began to build missile bases in Cuba. The U.S. Navy blockaded the island so that no more weapons could be brought in, and with the threat of nuclear war (the Cuban "missile crisis," it was called) horrifying the whole world, the Russians withdrew their missiles.

Shortly after Castro took over Cuba, the first wave of Cuban refugees arrived in Miami. The city of Miami is across a small bay from Miami Beach, the famous winter resort. Miami was the home of whites and blacks, mostly of Southern background, who ran the local government and worked in the resort hotels on the beach. At that time— some twenty years ago—Miami Beach was sliding downhill as a resort, and the city of Miami was decaying, too. Many of its residents were moving out into the suburbs.

That first wave of Cuban refugees was in large part people with education. They had professional and technical skills, and experience in business and administration. They were lawyers, doctors, accountants, engineers; they had had important jobs in publishing, design, manufacturing, importing. They left Cuba because the new Communist government had ended private ownership of property. No matter what their occupation, all Cubans now worked for the state. Under their system, private profits were impossible. Middle- and upper-class Cubans had the most to lose under Castro, so naturally they were the ones who wanted to emigrate.

What better place to make a new start than Florida? It was right next door. (It's just ninety miles from Havana to the Florida Keys.) The United States had the social and economic system these Cubans preferred; besides, many of them had been educated in American schools, and many had business connections here.

The United States opened its doors wide. It supplied the refugees with money and other aid to help them resettle. The effect was a quick boom in Miami. The enterprising Cubans started many business ventures. And the old, small Cuban-American community in Miami prospered as it moved to meet the housing and job needs of the newcomers.

As we saw with Rodolfo's story, some Cubans suffered hardship and prejudice at first. But in spite of this, most were soon making good in whatever they tried to do. The average Cuban-American family in Miami had an income slightly higher than that of the average non-Hispanic white family. One-third of all banking employees were Cubans, and Cubans controlled 40 percent of the construction business and made up 60 percent of the construction work force. Cubans also owned some 18,000 enterprises, most of them small service businesses. Their success drew investors from other Latin American countries. These Latin American businessmen felt more at home in the Hispanic atmosphere of the new Miami than in New York or other trade centers. Miami became not only a major business base, but a vacation spot for Latin American families.

Within twenty years, Greater Miami became a bilingual and bicultural community. Its Hispanic population grew from 6 percent in 1960 to 41 percent in 1980. Hispanics will soon be in the majority in Miami. Spanish, once a handy second language, is now the first language in the many parts of town that have become almost totally Cuban.

In the spring of 1980, another great wave of Cubans began to land on Florida's shores. Day after day, dozens of American fishing boats crossed the ocean to ferry heavy loads of refugees to Florida. Within a few months, over 125,000 Cubans had entered Florida without visas. During the previous year, Castro had allowed 100,000 exiles to make brief visits to Cuba. Word got around that he was again willing to let Cubans leave the island to join families in the United States. Cuban-Americans, anxious to be reunited with brothers, sisters, children, and parents, gladly paid anybody who could bring their relatives over.

Castro was apparently letting Cubans out to make things easier for himself. He was getting a subsidy of over a million dollars a day from Soviet Russia, but the Cuban economy was in bad shape. Natural disasters had struck hard. For two years running, plant blights had ruined Cuba's sugar, tobacco, and coffee crops. African swine fever had wiped out the nation's herds of hogs, and a Greek oil tanker had polluted the shellfish beds. All at once Cuba had nothing to trade with other countries for the food and materials she needed; and her most important meat source had been destroyed. This, added to the chronic problems of inefficient management, rigid bureaucracy, and low labor productivity caused many Cubans to turn away from the revolution and seek a better life abroad.

According to federal agencies, most of the new Cuban immigrants were healthy blue-collar workers, twenty to thirty years old. This wave of Cuban migrants was different from the earlier one in that it was younger and heavily male. About one person in ten was black. The majority of the migrants had trades, but they needed to learn English to fit into jobs. It turned out that only one in three really had family ties here.

A churchman who left Cuba long ago because he was "disillusioned by the revolution" returned for a visit and said he saw "some positive changes. You can't hide the truth. There have been advances in education and medicine since the revolution. And you don't see the same type of poverty that exists in other Latin American countries."

But for the young Cubans who came here in 1980, that was not enough. They were the first generation raised by the revolution. It had not won their devotion. Asked why they left the island, most of the new refugees said they wanted a better life. They complained of dull food, of lack of housing, of a scarcity of clothing and other consumer goods. Some also said their work did not satisfy

them, and they did not like the way everyone had to con-
form.

When the young Cubans met foreign tourists or Cuban
exiles who returned to Cuba for visits, they saw signs of
comfort and success not possible in Cuba. They wanted
to enjoy the middle-class life these visitors enjoyed. It was
a style they had heard about on the Voice of America's
radio broadcasts, and had seen on Spanish-language television programs that reached Cuba from Miami.

The Cuban-American community in Florida provided
money, clothing, and other essential articles to the newcomers. They offered jobs and opened their homes to
strangers, gave counseling and free medical care, and did
volunteer work in the many refugee services that sprang
up. Refugees who did not have relatives or jobs in Florida
were helped to get to places with sizable Cuban-American
communities, such as California, Oregon, New Jersey. Los
Angeles, which already had 100,000 Cubans, prepared to
receive another 10,000. For New York City, with its
110,000 Cubans, providing for the newcomers was hard.
The city has been losing jobs steadily, and has huge social
problems.

A year after the second wave of Cuban immigration took
place, reports on the newcomers' adjustment to American
life were still mixed. Gaspar Fernandez, who crossed in
a lobster boat in April 1980, told a reporter, "I am content.
This country has opened its arms to me. Others have not
done well, I know, but I have no cause for complaint."
He was trained as an accountant in Cuba; in New Jersey
he worked nights on the packing line of a vitamin plant.

Cubans who came to the U.S. in 1980 seeking a new life were helped by public or private agencies, or by family and friends already here. Nilda Nunez was one of the first to leave Cuba when Castro opened the door. Parents and a sister, who had come years earlier, gave her assistance. Here she joins three of her children at a playground near their home in Jackson Heights, New York. (Catherine Noren)

"That is the one thing we have learned," he said, "that you have to work hard in this country." But he also found his first winter in the North too cold, and hoped soon to join a friend in Miami who said job prospects there were good. Meanwhile, he was improving his English by watching soap operas each afternoon.

In Miami, the promise of a better life was dimming for many Cubans. "What is left a year later in this overwhelmed city," wrote a *New York Times* reporter, is "widespread bitterness and despair among the many refugees who have not received anything like the welcome they were promised." He found that over half the Cubans were making the slow adjustment to a new culture without complaints or mishap, helped by relatives and friends. But the refugees as a whole were often blamed for the few thousand who became involved in crime or disorderly behavior. "Each time I hear of something going wrong in Miami," said Enrique Calvo Martinez, "I expect to be castigated. I have not been disappointed." A teacher in Cuba, he had found work in Miami as a busboy.

School officials and social workers agreed that the new arrivals found it harder to adjust than the largely middle-class Cubans who came years before them. The reason offered was that the Communist system they grew up in seemed to have made them distrust personal ties; it weakened ambition and led people to try to beat the system rather than to work within it.

In the short run, prospects are not good, Miami civic leaders said. But most expect eventually to see conditions improve for the immigrants. "This is an exciting community," said one Miami official, "and we're changing every day. The old-timers might not realize it, but this is still the land of opportunity."

Less optimistic was Silvia Gonzalez, herself a Cuban refugee of 1959, and now head of the federal government's Cuban-Haitian Task Force office in Miami. She reports that the Cuban community fears another wave of immigration. "I don't think that this community could take it," she said. "I don't think this country could."

7

Ernesto's California

When Ernesto Galarza was a small boy, in the 1920s, his family left a mountain village in Mexico to try to make a living in California. Writing in his old age, Galarza recalled that time. The family's final stop was the city of Sacramento. Like other Mexicans fresh from the homeland, they headed straight for the barrio. There they could find a place to sleep, order a meal, buy overalls, and look for *trabajo* (work):

If work was action, the barrio *was where the action was. Every morning a parade of men in oily work clothes and carrying lunch buckets went up Fourth Street toward the railroad shops, and every evening they walked back, grimy and silent. Horse-drawn drays with low platforms rumbled up and down our street carrying the goods the city traded in, from kegs of beer to sacks of grain. Within a few blocks of our house there were smithies, hand laundries, a macaroni factory, and all manner of places where wagons and buggies were repaired, horses stabled, bicycles fixed, chickens dressed, clothes washed and ironed, furniture repaired, candy mixed, tents sewed, wine grapes pressed, bottles washed, lumber sawed, suits fitted and tailored, watches and clocks taken apart and put together again, vegetables sorted, railroad cars unloaded, boxcars iced, barges freighted, ice cream cones molded, soda pop bottled, fish scaled, salami stuffed, corn ground for masa, and bread ovened. To those who knew where these were located in the alleys, as I did, the whole* barrio *was an open workshop. The people who worked there came to know you, let you look in at the door, made jokes, and occasionally gave you an odd job.*

Once the Chicano had work, the next most important thing to do was to find a place to live that he could afford:

Ours was a neighborhood of leftover houses. The cheapest rents were in the back quarters of the rooming houses, the basements, and the run-down clapboard rentals in the alleys. Clammy and dank as they were, they were nevertheless one level up from the barns and tents where many of our Chicano *friends lived, or the shanties and lean-tos of the migrants who squatted in the "jungles" along the levees of the Sacramento and the American rivers.*

Barrio *people, when they first came to town, had no furniture of their own. They rented it with their quarters or bought a piece at a time from the secondhand stores, the* segundas, *where we traded. We cut out the ends of tin cans to make collars and plates for the pipes and floor moldings where the rats had gnawed holes. Stoops and porches that sagged we propped with bricks and fat stones. To plug the drafts around the windows in winter, we cut strips of corrugated cardboard and wedged them into the frames. With squares of cheesecloth neatly cut and sewed to screen doors, holes were covered and rents in the wire mesh mended. Such repairs, which landlords never paid any attention to, were made* por mientras, *for the time being or temporarily. It would have been a word equally suitable for the house itself, or for the* barrio. *We lived in run-down places furnished with seconds in a hand-me-down neighborhood all of which were* por mientras.

Like other immigrants, the Chicanos collected in neighborhoods where they could feel at home with their own. And they turned to their own folk for help:

They were continuously taking up collections to pay somebody's funeral expenses or to help someone who had had a serious accident. Cards were sent to you to attend a burial where you would throw a handful of dirt on top of the coffin and listen to tearful speeches at the graveside.

When newcomers arrived, if they had no money, they could count on those who had come before:

Beds and meals were provided—in one way or another—on trust, until the new Chicano *found a job. On trust and not on credit, for trust was something between people who had plenty of nothing, and credit was between people who had something of plenty. It was not charity or social welfare but something my mother called* asistencia, *a helping given and received on trust, to be repaid because those who had given it were themselves in need of what they had given. Chicanos who had found work on farms or in railroad camps came back to pay us a few dollars for* asistencia *we had provided weeks or months before.*

Because the barrio was a grapevine of job information, the transient Chicanos were able to find work and repay their obligations. The password of the barrio was trabajo, *and the community was divided in two—the many who were looking for it and the few who had it to offer. Pickers, foremen, contractors, drivers, field hands, pick and shovel men on the railroad and in construction came back to the barrio when work was slack, to tell one another of the places they had been, the kind of* patrón [boss] *they had had, the wages paid, the food, the living quarters, and other important details.*

There was a homey feeling in the barrio:

Within the barrio we heard Spanish on the streets and in the alleys. On the railroad tracks, in the canneries, and along the riverfront there were more Mexicans than any other nationality. And except for the foremen, the work talk was in our language. In the secondhand shops, where the barrio people sold and bought furniture and clothing, there were Mexican clerks who knew the Mexican ways of making a sale. Families doubled up in decaying houses, cramping themselves so they could rent an extra room to Chicano *boarders, who accented the brown quality of our Mexican* colonia.

It was at the family parties that the world of the Americans was completely shut off. . . . The host family prepared the tamales or the enchiladas, and everyone brought something for the feast. But these occasions were mainly for talking and not for eating. They were long parties, from late afternoon to midnight, the men in the front room, the mothers in the kitchen, the young women serving and whispering in the hall, the boys playing on the porch, and the babies put to bed all over the house.

When the case of beer arrived, the singing began. A guitar came down from a peg on the wall and those who could sing took turns with the ballads and the country love songs, the girls crowding the door to listen, the boys at the windows.

64

Ernesto's mother was a seamstress, but she could get little work. Nobody in the barrio had money for sewing. Ernesto's uncles, Gustavo and José, lived with them:

When they could, they worked on the riverfront, in the railroad shops, the canneries, lumberyards, pipe plants, stables, and nearby rice mills. When they couldn't, they rolled their clothes and blankets into bindles, hobo style, and walked the railway tracks to Woodland, Roseville, Stockton, Marysville, or Folsom for fruit picking, building construction, wood chopping, or sand hogging. When river traffic was at the peak in the summer and fall, they loaded grain on the barges or shipped as deckhands on the stern-wheelers that paddled between Colusa and San Francisco Bay. And one winter they walked to Truckee for a week's wages at a lumber mill.

We called it hacerle la lucha, *the daily match with the job givers, lay-offs, the rent, groceries, and the seasons. I was never told, and I never asked about getting into the* lucha. *I simply asked permission to do the* trabajos [jobs] *that I found, one by one, in the barrio.*

Ernesto was always looking for odd jobs a schoolboy could do. He ran messages for Western Union, he peddled newspapers, he played the fiddle at Saturday night dances, he decorated Christmas cards. And during summer vacations he went with other barrio people to the ranches to look for work:

In the labor camps I shared the summertime lives of the barrio people. They gathered from barrios *of faraway places like Imperial Valley, Los Angeles, Phoenix, and San Antonio. Each family traveling on its own, they came in trucks piled with household goods or packed in their secondhand* fotingos *and* chevees. *The trucks and cars were ancient models, fresh out of a used car lot, with license tags of many states. Into these jalopies much care and a good part of the family's earnings went. In camp they were constantly being fixed, so close to scrap that when we needed a part for repairs, we first went to the nearest junkyard. . . .*

Our main street was usually an irrigation ditch, the water supply for cooking, drinking, laundering, and bathing. In the better camps there was a faucet or a hydrant, from which water was carried in buckets and washtubs. If the camp belonged to a contractor and was used from year to year, there were permanent buildings— a shack for his office, the privies, weatherworn and sagging, and a few cabins made of secondhand lumber, patched and un-painted.

If the farmer provided housing himself, it was in tents pitched on the bare baked earth or on the rough, newly plowed land on the edge of a field. Those who arrived late for the work season camped under trees or raised lean-tos along a creek, roofing their trucks with canvas to make bedrooms. Such camps were always well away from the house of the ranchero, screened from the main road by an orchard or a grove of eucalyptus. I helped to pitch and take down such camps, on some spots that seemed lonely when we arrived, desolate when we left.

If you didn't have work, you spent the days looking for it. If you had it, Galarza said, you worried about how long it would last. It was best not to spoil your chances of being hired by asking questions about wages or food or housing or paydays:

Once we were in camp, owing the employer for the ride to the job, having no means to get back to town except by walking and no money for the next meal, arguments over working conditions were settled in favor of the boss. I learned firsthand the chiseling techniques of the contractors—how they knocked off two or three lugs of grapes from the daily record for each member of the crew, or the way they had of turning the face of the scales away from you when you weighed your work in.

There was never any doubt about the contractor and his power over us. He could fire a man and his family on the spot and make them wait days for their wages. A man could be forced to quit by assigning him regularly to the thinnest pickings in the field. The worst thing one could do was to ask for fresh water on the job, regardless of the heat of the day; instead of iced water, given freely, the crews were expected to buy sodas at twice the price in town, sold by the contractor himself. He usually had a pistol—to protect the payroll, so it was said. . . . We were certain that he had connections with the Autoridades, *for they never showed up in camp to settle wage disputes or listen to our complaints or go for a doctor when one was needed. Lord of a rag-tag labor camp of Mexicans, the contractor, a Mexican himself, knew that few men would let their anger blow, even when he stung them with curses.*

It was a long time ago that Ernesto Galarza came to the United States. He was a droplet in an unending stream of Mexican immigrants. Chicanos are a steadily growing part of the population of the Southwest. Today Ernesto's California has the largest Chicano population in the fifty states. Texas has the second largest Chicano population, and Arizona is next.

The Southwest is not the only area that draws people of Mexican origin. Mexican Americans account for over 1 percent of the population in Illinois, Kansas, Nevada, Utah, and Idaho. Great numbers of Chicanos also live in these heavily populated states: Michigan, Indiana, Ohio, Wisconsin, New York, Florida, and Washington. Actually, more Mexican Americans live in Illinois today than in either Colorado or New Mexico.

What explains the steady stream of Mexican immigrants? When did this migration begin, and why?

8

Across the Border

A generation before the English landed at Plymouth Rock, Mexican immigrants had settled in what is now New Mexico. Many of their descendants have never left New Mexico. No one except the Indians has lived longer in this country than the Mexicans. And since the 1930s, they have come into the United States in larger numbers than people of any other nationality. Today, over half of the six million people of Mexican origin in the United States are either first- or second-generation immigrants from Mexico. (A first-generation immigrant was born in Mexico. A second-generation immigrant was born in the United States, but at least one of his or her parents was born in Mexico.)

Two facts explain the steady stream of Mexican immigration. The first is the relative ease with which Mexicans can enter the United States. The second is the high standard of living in the United States.

The border between Mexico and the United States runs for almost two thousand miles. The eastern end is marked by a natural boundary, the Rio Grande River, which extends from the Gulf of Mexico to El Paso, Texas. The river wanders here and there, drops underground in places, and in time of drought stops flowing altogether. At some points it is easy to wade across the Rio Grande. Westward from El Paso, the border is only a surveyor's line, with no natural features to mark it. Some of it has been fenced in recent years. The towns along the border are split: one part of a town will be on American soil, the other on Mexican territory.

Such a border is not easily controlled. People can cross it fairly easily, either on their own or with the expert help of smugglers. Most of the Mexican immigrants come illegally.

Why are they so eager to cross the border?

The answer is money. Money not for luxuries or for pleasure—money for bread and milk, for medicines, for a coat and shoes, for a roof overhead and a bed to sleep in. Money to stay alive on, money to live decently.

Nowhere else in the world does a border separate two countries with so great a difference between the living standards of the people.

Let's compare the income of the average Mexican and the average American.

In 1978, the average Mexican's income was $1,244 a year.

That year, the average American's income was $8,612.

That's seven times as many dollars for the American. Even in times of inflation, the American's income can buy many, many more of the good things of life. Think what the Mexican could do with just some of those dollars to make life a little better, a little easier, for his family.

The Mexico the immigrants spring from was conquered by a Spanish adventurer, Hernando Cortez, in 1519. Cortez sailed from Hispaniola in search of wealth. He had heard stories about strange stone temples in the land called Mexico, and of the cotton clothing and gold ornaments worn by the Indians there. With five hundred soldiers, Cortez landed on the eastern shore of Mexico. His troops were armed with guns, swords, and spears. They had sixteen horses, sheathed in armor like the soldiers. The Aztec Indians feared the guns, and the horses, too, for they had never seen such animals. Cortez himself, they thought, might be the white god an Indian legend said would one day come to rule over them.

Because he did not wish to offend someone who might be a god, Montezuma, the Aztec ruler, did not rally an army to fight the Spaniards. Instead, he opened the gates of his capital, Tenochtitlán (today's Mexico City), to Cortez and his men. In time, the Spaniards conquered the Aztecs.

From the 1300s until the coming of Cortez, the Aztec Empire was one of the most thickly populated regions of the New World. From a stage of simple farming the Aztecs had developed intensive agriculture with large irrigation systems. Theirs was one of the most complex and wealthy civilizations of the Americas. The people were divided into many ranks and social classes: there were kings, nobles, and knights, and, below them, commoners, serfs, and slaves. The people the Aztecs conquered in tribal wars were enslaved. Indeed, it was some of these enslaved peoples who gladly turned against their masters to help the Spaniards take over Mexico. By brute force the Spaniards made Mexico a colony of Spain and enslaved the Indians who survived.

As news of the Aztecs' wealth spread, Spaniards poured out of other New World colonies to share in the looting of Mexico. In the years to come, the Spanish governors of Mexico sent out expeditions to explore the lands to the north and to plant settlements there.

The class system in Spanish Mexico was the same as in Puerto Rico, Cuba, and the rest of the Spanish Empire. Whites born in Spain, called *gachupines,* were the rulers. Whites born in Mexico, the criollos, or Creoles, became the aristocrats. But they held second place—in government, in business, in wealth. Both classes joined in the relentless effort to hold down the Indians, who were denied schooling, jobs, and personal liberties.

In Mexico, intermarriage between Creole men and Indian women produced a rapidly growing class called mestizos. A mestizo might also be part African, for the Spaniards had brought thousands of Africans to Mexico as slaves. The mestizos were treated almost as badly as the Indians.

In Mexico, the Indians were ground between two stones. The Catholic Church professed to save their souls, but did little for their day-to-day welfare. And the state, out to gather wealth, used the Indians as machines to be worked for the greatest profit.

Such a social system did little to expand the Mexican economy. The farms, ranches, and mines were all in the hands of a small minority. Agriculture never developed fully under the Spanish. The living standards of the mass of people remained low throughout the Empire's history.

In 1810, a revolt broke out; it was led by a Catholic priest, Miguel Hidalgo y Costilla, Its battle cry was "Independence and death to the Spaniards!" Taking heart from the examples of the American and French revolutions, the mestizos and Indians, who unlike the Creoles, had nothing to lose, struggled to free themselves from the Spanish yoke.

The war for independence lasted until 1821, when an independent Republic of Mexico was founded. The poor, however, enjoyed no benefits from the revolution. Again and again, military leaders grabbed power from one another by violent means. It was almost a century before the constant disorder ended.

Indeed, the government of Mexico underwent so many rapid and violent changes that it could exert little control over affairs in the northern reaches of the country. In the 1820s, Anglo-Americans were invited by the Mexican government to settle on the great prairies of what is now Texas. Conflict over slavery—the Anglos wanted it and Mexico opposed it—soon developed. The Anglo population grew and began to outnumber the Mexicans. Mexico tried but failed to stop further Anglo immigration. In 1836 Texas revolted against Mexican rule. The war that followed, the Texas Revolution, is probably best remembered for the dramatic Battle of the Alamo in San Antonio, which the Mexicans under Santa Anna won. In the end, however, Mexico lost the war, and the Anglos set up the independent Republic of Texas.

In 1845, the United States annexed Texas, adding it to the roster of slave states. The move was part of a Southern drive to expand slaveholding power. The cry for expansion of U.S. boundaries was entangled with the issue of slavery. The North feared that annexing Texas would add a new slave state to the Union and tilt the scales of political power against the free states.

At this critical moment President James Polk launched a war against Mexico. Ulysses S. Grant, who served in the Mexican War, called it the most disgraceful war the country ever fought. The army raised to battle the Mexicans contained many undisciplined volunteers who committed violent atrocities against Mexican civilians, including the crimes of murder, rape, and looting. General Winfield Scott, the head of the U.S. Army, later said his forces "committed atrocities to make Heaven weep and every American of Christian morals blush for this country."

The Mexican war was fought for no reason but to grab land that would expand slave territory. When Mexico lost, about half of all her land was taken away. A look at the map on page 5 shows how enormous her loss was. The United States acquired 850,000 square miles—more than the combined area of France, Spain, Germany, and Italy. Today this territory amounts to about one-third of the total area of the United States.

The peace terms were set down in the Treaty of Guadalupe Hidalgo, ratified in 1848. Mexico ceded to the United States not only the land, but also the 75,000 Mexican people living on it. Mexico insisted that full protection be given to both the property and the civil rights of her former citizens. But in spite of the guarantees in the treaty, the United States did not protect Mexican ownership of land. Through trickery, violence, or both, the land passed into the hands of Anglos. People of Mexican heritage became dependent upon Anglo landowners for a living.

Mexicans had long been considered by many white Americans to be an ignorant and inferior people. Now they carried the stamp of a conquered people. Although they were not formally enslaved, as the blacks had been, they were treated with the same contempt. This happened even though the Anglos in the Southwest were strongly influenced by the Mexican life-style and by Mexican customs.

Ranching was the way of life on the Southwestern frontier. There were three million head of cattle, sheep, goats, and horses in Texas at the time she won her independence. When the Republic of Texas was set up, many Mexicans fled their land there and left their herds behind. Anglos rounded up the abandoned cattle or raided Mexican ranches and stole cattle to begin their own herds.

The Texan Anglos had already learned the skills of ranching from the Mexicans. The Mexicans were the original cowboys, called *vaqueros*. The U.S. cattle industry developed out of the Mexican knowledge of breeding and pasturing. The *vaqueros* taught the Anglos how to ride, rope, trail, and brand. It was the *vaqueros* who invented the lariat, prime tool of the trade. The historian Laurence Seidman writes:

The Anglo-Americans adopted Mexican equipment, dress, and ranching methods. Many of the cowboy's terms, too, were Mexican. Corral, remuda, bronco, loco, sombrero, *were copied outright. Other Spanish words became corrupted because of the Texan's inabil-*

ity to pronounce them clearly. Lariat came from la reata, *the rope; rodeo from* rodear, *to surround with; pinto from* pinta, *a paint horse; lasso from* laso, *a slip knot or loop; chaps from* chaparreras, *leg armor; cinch from* cincha, *girth; ranch from* ranchero; *hoosegow from* jugado, *the prisoner's dock in a Mexican court; and stampede from* stampida, *meaning a crash or loud noise.*

Sheepherding was also developed by the Mexicans. And long before the Anglos came, the Mexicans had mastered many other skills the newcomers would borrow freely. The Mexicans knew how to irrigate dry lands and turn them into farming country. They knew how to mine copper and how to build adobe homes.

But in the end, the Mexicans' contributions brought them little share in the wealth of the southwest. The big cattle and sheep ranchers fenced in the land. Barbed wire shut out the small Mexican ranchers whose livestock had once fed on the open range. Slowly the Mexican sheepherders and cattlemen were wiped out.

Soon cotton planters moved into Texas, taking over still more of the land. After the U.S. Civil War, there were no longer black slaves to cultivate the crops, so landless Chicanos in need of work were taken on by the cotton growers as laborers or tenant farmers.

Fewer Mexicans lived in Arizona than in Texas. To feed the Anglo appetite for cheap labor, thousands of Mexicans were brought up from border towns. They worked on the cattle ranches and cotton plantations, and in the copper mines. Chicanos followed the mines as they opened and closed around the territory. In the company mining towns,

Chicano workers were rigidly separated from the Anglos by job, in housing, and even in the company stores, which had "Mexican" shopping hours.

The year the Treaty of Guadalupe Hidalgo was signed—1848—was the same year gold was discovered in California. Both events marked tremendous changes for Californian Mexicans. In the treaty, California was formally ceded to the United States. And in the Gold Rush of 1849, the Chicanos were overwhelmed by the wild rush of Anglos to the new territory. Thousands of Mexicans and Chileans came in, too, hoping to strike it rich. By the end of 1849 the population of California had jumped from 6,000 to 86,000.

To the Anglo gold miners from the South and the Midwest, Mexicans were all "greasers." The Mexican miners, "remote from any law," wrote one historian, "were taxed, lynched, robbed, and expelled in an endless series of incidents." Forced out of the mines, many Chicanos drifted into California towns, to become landless laborers.

The culture of the old California was gone. Any hope that Mexican and American might come together to make a new California was smashed by the miner's pick. Money-making became a mania. The ruthless exploitation of land, of natural resources, of people was a sickness that seized rural and urban life alike. "Progress," they called it, but it made life hell for thousands. Every minority was abused, insulted, humiliated, victimized by the new Anglo settlers. Chinese, Indian, black, Chicano—it made no difference. To many Anglos these people were all trash, scarcely human.

When the prospects of great wealth from mining rapidly faded, the Anglos turned to agriculture. They squatted on land that belonged to Mexicans. If the owners protested, the squatters took guns and drove them off. Within a few years the Chicanos lost most of the economic power they had had. The handful who survived as landowners were hated by their Anglo neighbors.

That was northern California, where the gold deposits were. In southern California, the Mexican *rancheros* held on to their land for a time. There were few Anglo settlers. But in the 1860s a terrible flood followed by a long, extreme drought ruined most of the rancheros. They could not pay their debts and lost their lands. When the railroads connected southern California with northern California and the East in the 1870s, it was the final blow. Anglo settlers rushed in by rail. After just one year the Chicanos in southern California, who had been in the majority, were outnumbered ten to one. Now bankers, railroad barons, and irrigation companies seemed to own everything. By 1900, Chicanos throughout California were reduced to the status of landless laborers.

Thomas Jefferson had dreamed of a life on the land for the greatest possible number of Americans. It was a dream that failed to come true in the southwest. Much of the land was swallowed up by the powerful few.

9

Pascual's Story

"Cheap labor!"

That was the need in the second half of the nineteenth century, and the Mexican worker supplied it. Railroads spun their steel web through the Southwest. They opened the region to great economic growth. Cotton plantations spread in California, Texas, and Arizona. Irrigation prepared the Imperial and San Joaquin valleys of California for rich fruit and vegetable crops. Mexican labor was needed even more when bans on Chinese immigration began in the 1880s and on the Japanese in 1907. World War I cut off the supply of European workers and then in the 1920s new laws put up barriers to mass immigration, laws from which Mexico and other nations of the Western Hemisphere were exempted.

Wages were low and work was hard, but still the Mexicans came. What other choice did they have? By 1900, about half the Chicanos in the Southwest were hired hands on farms. The majority of workers in railroads and mining were Chicanos, too. They built the roadbeds, laid the tracks, and were the section crews on the Santa Fe Line, the Rock Island, the Great Northern, the Southern Pacific. Many other Chicanos worked as servants and carpenters, clerks and waiters, laundresses and barbers.

By 1910, Chicanos were the main source of cheap labor for the Southwest. They crossed the border often and easily. There was no Border Patrol then, and U.S. immigration officials were hunting for illegal Asians, rather than Mexicans.

Before 1910, most of the Mexican migrants were temporary labor. The violent Mexican Revolution of 1910 changed the pattern. No longer bound to the land by debt, Mexican farm workers were free to move. Mexico's population had grown rapidly, and wages were too low to supply a family's needs. Across the border, wages were at least five times higher, and American businessmen were calling for more labor. So Mexicans migrated in even greater numbers.

In 1920 alone, 50,000 Mexicans came to the United States legally as "temporary" workers—but most stayed permanently. This was the usual pattern. The 1920s saw Chicanos move north and east to work in Chicago's and Kansas City's packing plants, on Detroit's auto assembly lines, in the steel mills of Ohio and Pennsylvania. The shift to urban life sped up, wages were higher, and the immigrants were learning skilled trades.

The flow of migrants slowed to a trickle during the Great

Depression of the 1930s. At the same time, Chicano families were encouraged—often forced—to return to Mexico.
About half a million went back. The Chicanos who stayed
went through terrible times, living in shacks, starving, dying of disease. Farm wages fell to fifteen cents an hour,
or worse. In California, migrants earned an average of
$250 a year. Chicano children as young as six worked in
the fields beside their parents. Many Chicanos in California
and the Southwest lost work altogether to Anglo migrants
fleeing the Dust Bowl, the farmlands of the Great Plains
states devastated by droughts and dust storms.

But with the coming of World War II, Chicanos again
found new places to work. As the armed forces drained
off millions of men, more jobs of all types opened up to
Chicanos. Many left the farms to work in airplane plants,
shipyards, and other war industries. The war gave some
Chicanos an opportunity of another kind. About half a
million of them served in the armed forces. They saw other
parts of the United States, and they saw many parts of
the world beyond—places where no one called them inferior. They learned new skills, they had new experiences,
they broadened their outlook. They became more aware
of themselves as a people, La Raza. Rodolfo "Corky" Gonzales described this new feeling in a poem:

La Raza!
Mejicano!
Español!
Latino!

81

Hispano!
Or whatever I call myself,
I look the same
I feel the same
I cry
and
Sing the same
I am the masses of my people and
I refuse to be absorbed. . . .
The odds are great
but my spirit is strong
      My faith unbreakable
      My blood is pure
I am Aztec Prince and Christian Christ
I SHALL ENDURE!
I WILL ENDURE!

The move of many people from the farms to the factories or to service in the armed forces resulted in a shortage of farm workers. So the U.S. Government worked out a program with the Mexican government to bring in a large supply of temporary farm workers. It was called the bracero program. (The word "bracero," based on the Spanish word for arms, *brazos,* literally means "one who works with his arms.") The United States promised decent living conditions and minimum-wage rates for the Mexican farm workers.

The bracero program was such a profitable deal for the farm owners that they got it extended for twenty-two years after its start in 1942. Each year, about half a million Mexican laborers came in for short periods of work. What the bracero program did was to push wages below what they

normally would have been. Low farm wages were one reason why Mexican Americans moved to the cities in even
greater numbers after World War II.

From 1950 to 1970, about 700,000 Mexican immigrants
entered the United States legally. This was in addition
to the millions of braceros brought in for short periods.
And in these decades, what was called the "wetback" tide
ran at full flood. ("Wetback" was the name applied to
workers who swam across the Rio Grande to avoid the
Border Patrol.) Over four million illegal migrants were
returned to Mexico by the U.S. Border Patrol, and there's
no knowing how many were not caught. The Border Patrol,
created in 1924, serves as the police force of the U.S.
Immigration and Naturalization Service (the INS).

What is life like today for Mexican migrant workers?
Pascual Jiminez Martinez lives in a shanty in Tijuana, Mexico, across the border from San Diego. Like tens of thousands of other Mexican laborers, he commutes daily to
work in the fields of the Anglos across the border. Pascual
now works for a tomato grower who signed a contract
with Cesar Chavez's United Farm Workers union. Fired
by the grower for trying to get his fellow workers to join
the union, Pascual joined Chavez as a volunteer union or-
ganizer. There was a nine-month strike before the field workers pressured the landowner into bargaining with them.

Pascual tells how it was for most migrant workers before
they organized into a union:

*Until March 1977, there was not one single company that was
giving the ten-minute break. Yet it is a state law. We filed complaints*

83

all over the place. We had no toilets or else dirty toilets. No drinking water. No wash water. Some workers had to live in caves, under trees, anywhere. In some migrant camps they slept in barracks, twenty to thirty stuffed in a room. Some were furnished blankets, some were not. If they had tortillas and beans, that was a lot. One day armed men in eight patrol cars—and with dogs—converged on us. Growers had the power to use the police to intimidate us.

Workers were picking crops from 7:00 A.M. to 9:00 P.M. with no guarantee of wages, no medical plan, no grievance procedures against firings for union organizing. We were treated like animals, and we would be loaded on flatbed trucks with no guardrails and hauled to various fields at incredible speeds. Several workers fell and broke their legs and arms. Foremen abused and shouted at workers: "Animals, let's go!" Now with the union, people are less afraid to protest.

The hardest part of field work, Pascual said, was taking insults:

A worker is usually so beaten down by insults he can't stand up for his rights. But we've gained a few privileges now, and they mean so much: a jug from which you can get a cup of water, having the use of a clean toilet. Before the foreman would say, "You Mexicans will get sick at your stomach if you drink the water on this side." Once we said we'd like to pool some money and get some ice. It was our money. But he said, "Oh no, you will get sick in the head if you have ice."

Workers at the end of the day like to change into clean clothes. But Bobby, the boss, didn't see it that way:

We had the use of an old shed, but one day Bobby locked it, saying, "I need it for storage." We took it up with the union, and the union ruled a grower could not remove rights or privileges we previously had enjoyed, and Bobby had to unlock the shed. We still have a problem with him. We want to eat something hot or cold, to have a commercial food wagon pass by once during the day. But they can only come if the grower okays it. And Bobby said, "No way. You'll be eating and talking and I'll be losing time."

Grace Halsell is a reporter who worked in the fields alongside Pascual and many other migrants. She found a remarkable spirit among them:

Back in the rows, one worker starts to sing. Another joins him and then a third. Others listen to small radios they carry around their waists. Always there is joking. They have a spirit, a goal, a unity, and a caring, one for the other, that is like a religious experience. I have not known such a feeling since the religious revival meetings I attended as a child. Their striving for a better life is infectious. Despite burdens that have destroyed millions of others, the survivors exude confidence and even a sense of joy.

Many Anglos, she says, would not understand a man like Pascual. As an American citizen (he was born in California while his father and mother were working there), why does he remain in this hard and dirty field work? Couldn't he better himself? Move on up the economic ladder? Grace Halsell says he sees it differently from the Anglo. The dollar does not come first. "Being is more important than achieving."

Pascual did try other jobs. Once he worked in an electronics plant. He made more than double what he makes in the fields. But he did not like being in a windowless plant all day. He likes farm work:

Even in the rain. Or when it's cold. Or when it's hot. I like sowing the seeds, setting out small plants. [He says the workers treat the plants like babies.] We build stakes to protect them. We tie the plants around the stakes. And we trim the plants when they grow tall. I like being near the earth. I like the smell of the air, of the plants. I like to see the sky. I am not happy staying inside a building all day. All of nature is shut out. I feel I lose my time. And I am happy when I come to the fields. The work is too hard. But gracias a Dios [*thank God*] *I am able to do it.*

The great majority of Mexican immigrants who remain in the United States start out poor and remain poor. In the Southwest, Mexican Americans have much smaller incomes than Anglos. Throughout the country, Mexican Americans make less than members of most other ethnic groups. Because Chicano families are usually large, the earnings of the head of the household must be stretched a long way. Chicano wives often must stay at home to care for their young children, and so do not contribute to the family income.

Among groups usually thought of as "disadvantaged," Chicanos are about in the middle. The average income of a black, Native American, or Puerto Rican family is even lower than that of a Chicano family, while, on the average, Cubans and Asian Americans are better off.

In 1950, two out of three people of Mexican ancestry (67 percent) lived in cities. Today, more than four out of five (80 percent) live in cities. A million Chicanos live in Los Angeles—only Mexico City has a higher concentration of Mexicans. There is a significant difference between the incomes of Chicanos who live in cities and the incomes of those in rural regions. The city people are much better off, especially if they live outside the Southwest.

The percentage of Chicanos who are truly poor is higher than the percentage of Anglos in this category. (But blacks are worse off yet.) In 1960, one out of three Chicano families—33 percent—fell below the "poverty line"; in 1970, this figure had gone down slightly, to 25 percent. Still, we can see that if the Chicano's chance to earn a livable wage has improved, it has done so very slowly.

For the poorest Chicanos, the effects of poverty are plain in every aspect of daily life. The soaring price of gasoline means the poor cannot afford to drive long distances to work. Rising food prices mean even less, and worse, food on the table. Bad housing deteriorates further and becomes more overcrowded. In rural areas, many Chicano families live in shacks, often without plumbing or electricity. The poor Hispanic neighborhoods mirror the poverty of their people and the failure of community agencies to respond to their needs: streets are unpaved; curbs, sidewalks, and streetlights disappear; junked cars, uncollected garbage, and burned-out buildings are depressingly familiar sights. With poverty and feelings of hopelessness come high rates of crime and heavy use of illicit drugs. Heedless of the way the poor feel about their old neighborhoods, government authorities tear down tenements and scatter the inhabitants to make way for freeways.

Poor nutrition and overcrowded conditions foster illness

and early death, too. Chicanos in Houston and San Antonio are much more likely to die at an early age than the Anglos of those cities.

The living conditions of most Puerto Ricans in the United States are just as bad as those of Chicanos; sometimes they are even worse. Indeed, *most* Hispanics in this country live in poverty—people from Ecuador, Guatemala, Bolivia, and other Latin American nations are unable to earn a decent living, get decent housing, or buy enough food to feed their families well. Some of the Cubans, as we have seen, are somewhat better off, but they, too, may live in poor neighborhoods and have to struggle to get by.

Why should this be, when the United States is such a rich nation? What keeps such a large segment of our population so poor?

The answer, simply put, is "Discrimination." People have discriminated against one ethnic minority after another throughout the history of this country. It is easy to name the reasons for this, but not so easy to understand them. Let's take a look at one of those reasons: racism.

10

Pictures Can Lie

Going to the movies is fun. And in Bernardo Vega's first years in New York, during the 1920s, it was also cheap. Ten cents would get you into the theaters on East 86th Street, in the German neighborhood where Vega and his friends lived.

But he noticed that whenever the story was set in a foreign land, it followed the same pattern:

If the scene was supposed to be Mexico, then the screen was filled with sombreros and lazy, sleep-eyed men who would wake up to shoot it out and then go back to sleep. . . . All foreigners were bandits. The South American countries were inhabited by savages. Only the hero—a Yankee, of course—was clean, generous, brave, always ready to take blows in defense of the poor innocent girl who in the end fell into his arms.

When the movie dealt with his own country, Puerto Rico, it was the same thing:

Wild boys climbed coconut trees like a bunch of monkeys. Women without shoes and wrapped in hides would walk along mountain trails with huge baskets of tropical fruit, while the men would be fast asleep in the shade. There were alligators fighting in a lagoon and snakes basking in the warm sun. And the shining Yankee good-guy would overcome all dangers to save the native girl longing to be taught the arts of North American civilization.

Those films were not fun for Bernardo Vega. They were painful. Hollywood in its movies was spreading distorted notions of what Hispanic people were like. Such images are called "stereotypes." They pop up frequently in movies, television shows, magazines, newspapers. You come across them in popular songs, in comic strips, in children's books, in novels. You hear jokes based on stereotypes about Poles, Jews, blacks, Puerto Ricans.

Even the best writers may perpetuate stereotypes. John Steinbeck, an American novelist who won the Nobel Prize for literature, once wrote a story called *Tortilla Flat*. It dealt with Chicanos who lived on a hill above Monterey, California. Steinbeck painted a picture of these people as soaked in cheap wine, sleeping in ditches, fighting for the fun of it, stealing everything in sight, and making love to anyone and everyone. Only later did he realize how harmful that novel was; then he apologized for it.

Stereotypes are bad because they generalize about a group of people who are individuals, with all the differences found in any group. Stereotypes represent all the people in a group as alike, exactly the same. Examples: Jews are crooks, blacks are dope fiends, Chinese are sly, the Irish are drunks, Germans are humorless.

This doesn't mean all generalizations are wrong. For example, it's true that most mushrooms are not good eating. And it's right not to serve ham and beer if the guests you have invited are vegetarians, Hindus, Orthodox Jews, and Black Muslims.

Not all stereotypes are negative, either. Some are favorable—but they are just as wrong when they are applied uniformly to everyone in a group. Examples: blacks have musical ability, Jews are smart, Germans are clean, Americans have know-how, Asians are polite. These stereotypes are less hurtful, but they are still a false substitute for real knowledge of individual people.

Usually we get our image of people outside our own group from what we've heard or read—in folklore, in the mass media, in church, in books—and not through personal contact. Then, too, our first contact with someone different or strange may have a big effect on our overall image of that person. Someone's differences may seem threatening or funny to us because we know so little about the person. This may happen especially if the differences are very noticeable—for example, if someone's skin is a different color from ours, or if someone does not speak our language well.

We know that if a group is the victim of stereotyping, it doesn't mean those in the group do not stereotype other people. And sometimes the victims of a negative stereotype even begin to believe in the stereotype themselves. This can happen if the stereotype has been ground in by ceaseless repetition.

Where do such stereotypes come from?

They are the result of racism.

Racism is the false belief that some "races" are superior and other "races" are inferior. One group is supposed to be born superior—everyone in the group is bright, wise, talented, strong. And another group is supposed to be born inferior—everyone in it is stupid, weak, lazy, vicious.

Modern science has junked such ideas. It has demonstrated that no classification of races holds up. No one has ever shown scientifically that "race" explains anything about a group of people. There are simply no innate differences in ability or character from one racial or national group to another. But racism goes back a very long way, and the false idea that some groups are naturally superior is hard to get rid of.

In the baggage the first white explorers carried to the New World was the belief that their white skin made them superior. In the minds of these white people, colored people were inferior. These whites identified red people and black people with evil, with savagery. The racist beliefs gave white colonists an excuse for enslaving Africans, for killing Native Americans. Colored people were good only for doing the hard and dirty work the white man did not want to do.

These racist beliefs were woven into custom and law, into religion and education. Each white generation learned from preacher and teacher that colored peoples were inferior. There was nothing wrong with enslaving and mistreating inferiors. It was "natural" and "necessary" to segregate them, to discriminate against them.

A harsh selfishness has marked the treatment of colored peoples. Native Americans were ruthlessly exploited from the beginning. And later, those who had not been exterminated were herded onto reservations. The Africans were enslaved, and after Emancipation the gains made during the brief years of Reconstruction were steadily taken away. The Chinese in the West were sweated in the mines and in the building of the railroads, and then were shut out of America completely by the Chinese Exclusion Act of 1882. The Japanese-Americans, citizens and noncitizens alike, were penned up in U.S. concentration camps during World War II. In Europe, during the same war, Hitler and the Nazis murdered six million Jews because, the Nazis said, though they were white, they were nevertheless an inferior race who should be exterminated, like rats or germs.

So stereotypes are the result of prejudice. They tend to justify prejudice, and they certainly strengthen it. It is worthwhile to try to get rid of stereotypes, though that alone would not tear up the roots of prejudice. Still, once you become aware of stereotypes, you can spot them for what they are and figure out the ways in which they don't make sense. "Chicanos are lazy and irresponsible," people say. Yet it is the Chicano's willingness to work hard that makes the Anglo boss seek him out when there is hard labor to be done at low wages.

We could say that many stereotypes are lies. You may

tell a lie if you are afraid to tell the truth. Stereotypes are also based partly on fear.

Immigrants to America, white or colored, have always been distrusted and feared—partly because they are different, partly for other reasons. The feelings of fear and distrust have led to stereotyping of the newcomers.

When the Irish began coming in large numbers, before the Civil War, they triggered anti-Catholic hysteria in what was then a largely Protestant nation. "The Pope is scheming to seize the United States!" cried the newspapers. The Irish, who arrived poor, were called vicious brutes. They did the dirtiest and hardest work, struggling to make decent lives for themselves.

Then, in the 1880s, a new flood of immigrants began pouring in from eastern and southern Europe. The Anglo-Americans' distrust of newcomers was renewed. This time it was not one but a *dozen* different ethnic groups arriving. Their strange languages, religions, customs, and politics again made the dominant white Anglo-Saxon Protestants fearful and hostile. They said the newcomers were inferior people. They would not fit into American life, and, disappointed and angry, would overturn the government by bloody revolution.

Personal differences are not all that cause hostility to newcomers. In hard times, people are afraid they will lose what they have. So, during times of depression, working people resent immigrants who compete with them for the few jobs available. And any rise in immigration is perceived as a threat by wage earners who came to the United States earlier. These workers fear that poor and unskilled immigrants will work for very little and take their jobs or lower

their pay. Labor unions, therefore, have objected to unlim-
ited immigration more than once in the past. Union leaders
have sometimes made a point of *not* recruiting recent immigrants, claiming it would be too difficult to organize people
who speak foreign languages. Keeping newcomers out of
the unions has served to keep them out of good union
jobs. Immigrants have sometimes become "scabs," taking
the jobs of workers on strike. Union members bitterly resent this, but the unions must share the blame for this
situation if they have not tried to recruit the immigrants.

When Hispanic newcomers first meet up with discrimination, they find it very confusing. Cubans, Puerto Ricans,
Mexicans, and all other Hispanics have a broad history
of racial intermingling. As we have seen, they are partly
Native American, partly European, and partly African.
Members of a single Hispanic family will often display as
wide a variety of racial characteristics as Hispanics do as
a group. When reporters asked hundreds of Hispanics in
New York about their race, three out of four refused to
identify themselves as black or white. Their nationality or
cultural background was what mattered to them, not their
color.

Whatever race Anglos consider Hispanics to be, it is
an "inferior" one. "If you work hard, you can become a
success," runs the common American belief. But "you
don't get ahead just by working hard," says a Puerto Rican
educator, the president of a community college in New
York. "Something outside of you determines just how far
you will get. You must *demand* that the outside recognize
your assets."

That "outside" is the world of the dominant majority—

the Anglo world. There racism operates daily. Hispanics come to the States because there are jobs to be filled, because their labor is needed. Many of them are unskilled and qualify only for poor jobs at low pay. At the same time, on-the-job training and other types of advancement are denied them. Racism provides an excuse for this kind of exploitation by saying, in effect, Hispanics are good for nothing else. It makes possible greater profits from the cheap labor of an oppressed people.

What Hispanic Americans are up against is much more than racism practiced by individuals. It is institutionalized racism. By that I mean the major institutions of American society—corporations, banks, courts, the police, the press, unions, schools, churches, the armed services—discriminate on racial grounds. Sometimes they do it knowingly, sometimes not. But the result of being treated as an inferior is to be sentenced to a life of poverty and pain.

To see how it works for Hispanics not in theory, but in real life, let's look at the Chicanos. In the Southwest, Chicanos were expected to live in the barrios, or ghettos. They were kept out of places of recreation—public parks, playgrounds, swimming pools—supposedly open to everyone. They could get only the most menial and unskilled jobs, even when they were well-qualified for better ones. In some places they could go only to segregated schools and segregated movie theaters. The police were quick to use violence against Chicanos, and often ignored their civil rights. In Texas, where discrimination was the worst, restaurants refused to serve Chicanos, kindergarten teachers called children "greasers," churches held separate services

"For Colored and Mexicans." The Anglo view of Chicanos was expressed in what a Texas farmer said to a reporter: "You can't mix with a Mexican and hold his respect. It's like the nigger; as long as you keep him in his place, he is all right."

During World War II, two things happened in Los Angeles that show how powerful prejudice against Chicanos was. In 1942, a gang of teenage Chicano boys was arrested and tried for murder. The verdict was guilty even though the prosecutor produced no evidence in court to prove his case. Local prejudice was so strong that it was enough simply to accuse Chicano boys of a crime for a jury to convict them. The boys spent two years in San Quentin prison, waiting for their appeal to be heard. The higher court unanimously reversed the lower court's decision "for lack of evidence." And reprimanded the judge for his prejudiced behavior during the trial.

In the next year, 1943, the famous "Zoot Suit Riots" made the front pages of the national press. At that time, the style among Chicano youth was to wear what they called "zoot suits." A zoot suit had baggy pants with a high waist and tight cuffs, and a long coat with wide shoulders and a loose back; it was worn with a broad-brimmed flat hat. One night some sailors were attacked while wandering through the barrio of Los Angeles. The sailors claimed their attackers had been Chicanos. The police came in, but found no one to arrest. The next night, two hundred sailors went into the barrio and took the law into their own hands. They beat up every zoot suiter they ran across. The police did nothing to stop the sailors. On the next

97

few nights, sailors, soldiers, and Marines stalked the Los Angeles streets, cornering Chicanos and savagely beating them. *Time* magazine called it "the ugliest brand of mob action since the coolie race riots of the 1870s." Not until the Mexican government put pressure on the U.S. State Department to curb military leaves in Los Angeles did the mob violence stop.

These dramatic examples go back some forty years in time. But despite the passage of Civil Rights laws in the 1950s and 1960s, injustice to the Chicano has not stopped. There are endless stories of police brutality—and sometimes the violence ends in death. The Chicano community hears about such cases, but the Anglo world blots the news out. A Dallas policeman shoots and kills a small boy after picking him up "on suspicion." A California boy is shot to death while "resisting arrest." A man "chokes himself to death" in prison while awaiting trial. Police make dragnet arrests of Chicanos as a standard procedure. The 1970 report of the U.S. Commission on Civil Rights concluded that "there is evidence of a widespread pattern of police misconduct, including incidents of excessive police violence, discriminatory treatment of juveniles, and excessive use of 'arrests for investigation' and 'stop and frisk.' " The commission's findings referred not only to Hispanic people but to minorities in general.

The Texas Rangers are notorious for harassing Chicanos. The Border Patrol has a reputation for rude and often violent treatment of Mexican Americans. The Border Patrol has an enormous job to do, but its way of doing it has given it a bad reputation.

It is no wonder that Hispanics and other minorities distrust public agencies. When they need to seek the help of such an agency—for education, job training, welfare benefits, health care, legal aid, immigration visas, work permits—they approach it with suspicion. Cultural differences account for this in part, and of course language is often a barrier. But mainly, Hispanics are wary of public agencies because they expect the agencies to discriminate against them. The Anglos are in charge, and too often treat Hispanics like second-class citizens.

11

"We Will Not Lose What Is Ours "

Luis Chávez is the father of nine children. He lives in a two-bedroom shack near a small Texas town not far from the Mexican border. He could live in a better house, he says, but he saves every cent he can so his children may have a better education.

In the Rio Grande Valley, where the Chávezes live, work is hard to get during the summer because so many Mexicans cross the border for jobs. So early in July the Chávez family migrates north to work in Michigan for four months. There they live in one-room shacks in labor camps, sometimes with one bathroom for two hundred people.

They wait to go until July so that the Chávez children can finish the school term in Texas. Luis, who went to school only one day in his whole life, speaks no English. He wants a better life for his nine children.

The Chávez family testified before the U.S. Civil Rights

Commission studying the problems of migrant labor. Cruz Reynoso, a staff lawyer, asked Luis's son José if his high school encouraged students to go on with their education. The school is about 90 percent Mexican-American.

JOSÉ: Most of the time when a student has a problem in school, he tries to go to the counselor, but she always tells you that she is too busy, she will get back to you later. Instead of going back again you just stay with it. . . .

REYNOSO: How many counselors do you have at this school?

JOSÉ: One.

REYNOSO: How many students are there?

JOSÉ: About 1,100.

REYNOSO: Has there been some concern with respect to getting advice as to going to college and that sort of thing, in addition to plain counseling at the high school?

JOSÉ: Most of the time the students that I have talked with say that the teacher says the opportunities are there to go to college which she doesn't talk about it too much to us.

REYNOSO: So the young people in high school don't know anything about the opportunities?

JOSÉ: Most of them don't.

REYNOSO: Do you yourself hope to go on with your education if you make it through high school okay?

JOSÉ: Yes, I do . . . I would like to be a mathematics teacher.

Of course, there are always those teachers who truly care about their students—*all* their students, no matter who they are or where they came from. Ernesto Galarza went to Lincoln School in Sacramento. He remembers what his principal, Miss Hopley, did for the students:

Miss Hopley and her teachers never let us forget why we were at Lincoln: for those who were alien, to become good Americans; for those who were so born, to accept the rest of us. Off the school grounds we traded the same insults we heard from our elders. On the playground we were sure to be marched up to the principal's office for calling someone a wop, a chink, a dago, or a greaser. The school was not so much a melting pot as a griddle where Miss Hopley and her helpers warmed knowledge into us and roasted racial hatreds out of us.

At Lincoln, making us into Americans did not mean scrubbing away what made us originally foreign. The teachers called us as our parents did, or as close as they could pronounce our names in Spanish or Japanese. No one was ever scolded or punished for speaking in his native tongue on the playground. Matti told the class about his mother's down quilt, which she had made in Italy with the fine feathers of a thousand geese. Encarnación acted out how boys learned to fish in the Philippines. I astounded the third grade with the story of my travels on a stagecoach—which nobody else in the class had seen except in the museum at Sutter's Fort. After a visit to the Crocker Art Gallery and its collection of heroic paintings of the golden age of California, someone showed a silk scroll with a Chinese painting. Miss Hopley herself had a way of expressing wonder over these matters before a class, her eyes wide open until they popped slightly. It was easy for me to feel that becoming a proud American, as she said we should, did not mean feeling ashamed of being a Mexican.

Some Hispanic children today undoubtedly have the same happy experiences Ernesto Galarza had at Lincoln School. But, overall, American public schools have done a dismal job of educating Hispanic children. All the figures on dropouts and on low achievement among Hispanic students show this.

There are exceptions. While Puerto Ricans, Chicanos, and the children of immigrants from many other Latin American countries have been even more poorly educated than blacks, the Cubans in Florida have done better. But the Cubans, until 1980, were mostly middle-class and professional people, already well educated when they came to the States. So their situation was different.

In the Southwest, Chicanos have been handicapped in seeking better jobs because their education has been so poor. On the average, they have several years' less schooling than Anglos. People with less than a tenth-grade education do not stand much of a chance in the world of work or business. In the last few decades, the gap between Chicanos and Anglos has been closing. The youngest generation, especially, has had more schooling. But, in general, American schools fail to hold Chicanos; more blacks and many more Anglos go on to high school and college.

If a school system educates one minority badly, the system almost certainly educates the others badly too. The more segregated a school system is, the poorer the record of the Chicano students. The fact that there are very few Chicano teachers is important, too. There are few of them because in the past so few Chicano children were graduated from high school and went on to college. In the Southwest, until recently, there was one Anglo teacher for every 30 Anglo students, one black teacher for every 39 black students, and one Chicano teacher for every 120 Chicano students.

The money spent on educating Chicano students is another measure of discrimination. The more Chicanos there are in a school district, the less money the school district spends on education. This also means that the teachers get less pay than teachers in predominantly Anglo districts.

The picture is much the same for Puerto Rican students in mainland schools. One study showed that nearly 70 percent of Puerto Rican students in ghetto schools read at a badly retarded rate—the figure is half that, 35 percent, for students in non-ghetto schools. "Why hang around when it's doing no good?" say Puerto Rican students as they drop out of school. Half the Puerto Rican students who reach the eighth grade drop out by the twelfth grade. At the age of sixteen, when schooling is no longer compulsory, there is a great wave of departures. The majority of young Puerto Ricans never get a high school diploma. What's left for them? Only poorly paid, unskilled jobs— or no jobs at all.

Hardworking Hispanic parents do their best to see their children through school. Today, more Hispanic students are graduating from high school, and some do go on to college. But so few get higher education, compared to the rest of the population! Only 1 percent of the total Chicano population, and only 1.3 percent of the Puerto Rican population, goes to college. (By comparison, 2 percent of blacks go to college.) And these figures are for the early years of college. Recently, colleges have made an effort to increase minority freshman enrollment. But some minority students fail to make it, and leave college before graduating.

No wonder it is hard for Hispanic students to do well in school! Many American schools deny Hispanic students the use of their own language. They do not teach pride in the Hispanic heritage—in fact, the community is often hostile to and ignorant of Hispanic culture, and the schools reflect this. The Anglo-American majority knows little or nothing about the Spanish language and culture. Though Mexico is our next-door neighbor, few schools teach its history. Mexico is mentioned only when Texas and the Mexican War of 1846–48 come up. Puerto Ricans are U.S. citizens, but the island's history gets short shrift in the textbooks. While Latin America as a whole has long been a source of profit for U.S. businesses, schools usually treat Latin America like an unwelcome neighbor. When textbooks deal with Latin America at all, the story is told from the Anglo point of view. The Anglos often turn out to be the clever heroes and the Latinos the stupid cowards or villains—the stereotypes at work again. Sometimes, rather than stereotyping Hispanic groups, the textbooks and novels read in school leave them out altogether.

It's hard to develop pride in yourself and your people when this happens. Hispanics often feel like strangers in U.S. schools. Their difficulty with the English language often seals their lips and their minds. They feel lost. The less they learn, the more they despair. All but the strongest, the brightest, and the luckiest quit.

Language is the greatest problem for Hispanic students. They are loyal to their native tongue. No foreign language has been so strongly held on to in this country as Spanish. Fully half the people in the United States who speak some language other than English in the home speak Spanish. Relatives and friends here in the United States naturally use Spanish to communicate with recent immigrants, but as a matter of tradition, too, Hispanics keep speaking Spanish generation after generation. Hundreds of radio stations and dozens of television stations that broadcast some or all of the time in Spanish help to keep up the use of Spanish throughout the country. There are also many American newspapers in Spanish.

Hispanics know that a command of English is necessary if they hope to get ahead. But they insist that they also want to retain Spanish and their Hispanic culture. Why should they have to choose between the two? There are so many Hispanic Americans now that their needs and desires demand attention. School enrollment alone tells the dramatic story. In San Antonio, Hispanic children now make up 52 percent of the school population; in Hartford, Connecticut, 35 percent; in Denver, 31 percent; in New York City, 30 percent; in Los Angeles and Miami, they are now the largest group in the public schools.

Decisions on how best to educate such a large part of the population are important to the whole country. Not only to see that Hispanic children get the good education they deserve, but to make sure that the human dignity and worth of generations of children are not wasted.

The right to speak one's own language is certainly a basic human right. From World War I until recently, that right has usually been denied in American schools. Yet one thing that might help Hispanic students immensely is bilingual education. Many people mistakenly believe that instruction in two languages would be something new in the public schools. But as far back as 1840 schools in Cin-

cinnati offered instruction in German to pupils who understood no English. New York City schools have taught foreign-born children in German, Yiddish, Italian, and Chinese. It was during World War I, when anti-German feeling ran so high, that bilingual education was stopped. In many states, all use of foreign languages before the eighth grade was forbidden.

It was the flood of Cuban refugees into Florida in the early 1960s that revived bilingual education. The schools in the Miami area had to find ways to teach the refugee children. They gave instruction in Spanish until the students were able to learn in English. And that method spread elsewhere. Texas and New Mexico used it with Chicano newcomers. But not all school systems believe they can afford bilingual education, and not all educators think it is a good thing.

The aim of bilingual education, very simply, is to help students whose mother tongue is not English. There are now over five million children in the United States whose first language is not English. They speak dozens of other languages. About 70 percent of these children are Hispanic. Most live in homes in which Spanish is spoken some of the time or all the time.

Bilingual education presents a pupil's subject matter—science, arithmetic, history, and all the rest—in his or her native tongue. As the student goes along, more and more material is introduced in English. At the same time, the student gets special help in learning English, so that eventually he or she can switch entirely into regular classes.

This is the federal government's view of bilingual education. Some educators have come up with their own way to do the job. They want the freedom to try their own method. Students who don't speak English are put into regular classes and are given special daily instruction in the basics of English through a program known as "English as a second language." The backers of this program say that most students make such rapid progress in English that it isn't necessary to teach the regular subjects in their native language. But those who support "classic" bilingual education answer that most students are bound to fall behind during the period when they are just learning English.

In any case, bilingual education is not an easy thing to manage. Schools have to determine which students need it, figure out what kind of programs to give them, and decide when the students are ready to be placed in regular classes. They also have to find bilingual teachers, and this is not always easy.

Today, about 800,000 children in the United States are getting some form of bilingual education. Experts differ over how well bilingual education is working. Some say it has not been very helpful. Others say the results have not been measured properly, or that it is too early to judge. They think bilingual education should be continued until its effects on students can be determined more accurately. Still other critics ask how the schools can afford the cost of bilingual education. It might add $200 million to $600 million to the yearly cost of public education.

The critics of bilingual education say they are not against giving special attention to students whose first language is not English. The argument is not over *whether* something

This art display in a corridor of P.S. 189 in New York is the product of bilingual education at the school. Before it could be firmly established nationally, bilingual education was threatened by economic crises and changes in political policy. (Catherine Noren)

should be done for these students, but over *how* it should be done.

The important thing, of course, is to make it easier for Hispanic children to find their way in an American school. In the late nineteenth and early twentieth century, when immigrants arrived by the millions every year, their children were usually thrown into the public schools—it was sink or swim. Some of those who "made it" under those conditions say, "Why can't today's newcomers do it the way we had to?" But they forget how many immigrant children failed to "swim" in the "good old days." Colin Greer, a historian of education, writes, "The truth is that our public schools have always failed the lower classes—both white and black."

It is a great sign of progress that, in 1974, the U.S. Supreme Court ruled unanimously that special education must be provided for children whose primary language is not English. (The case the Supreme Court ruled on was Lau vs. Nichols; it involved the rights of Chinese children in San Francisco.) The court did not propose specific ways to provide the special education. For some time now, the Department of Education and Congress have been debating how the job should be done and how much federal money to spend on it.

Hispanics see bilingual education as a means of fighting discrimination and improving their chances of better jobs. They want bilingual programs to teach Hispanic history and culture. Chicanos, Puerto Ricans, Cubans, and other Hispanics are loyal to a shared mother tongue, and they want their children to grow up knowing who they are.

"Spanish gives us identity and emotional security," says Augustin Gonzalez, director of the Puerto Rican Family Institute in New York. "Past migrations lost their language, and this caused them much emotional damage. Our culture is very strong, and we will not lose what is ours."

12

Farm Workers on Strike

It was twenty years ago that Cesar Chavez began slowly to build a community among migrant farm workers of the West. It would become a union, the United Farm Workers, now part of the AFL–CIO. Nonviolence was the moral path its members chose in seeking social change. "If you muster enough power, you can move things. Power is needed to get justice," says Chavez. "The only way you can generate power is by doing a lot of work." Over the years the union learned how to use political power to help people solve their problems.

The famous grape strike, led by Chavez, began in 1965 when the union had scarcely a thousand members and only $82 in its treasury. For five long and painful years the strike tested the farm workers' endurance and strength. In the end they won recognition as a union but the "end" was only a beginning. "Work for social change and against social injustice is never ended," says Chavez. "The whole

Banners flying from the barricades put up by strikers to stop trucks from moving in and out of a packing plant.

fight, if you're poor and you're a minority group, is for economic power. We want radical change—sufficient to control our own destinies."

These photographs show glimpses of the farm workers during a recent strike in California.

(Photographs in this chapter by Morrie Camhi)

Picketing the truck parking lot at the packing plant.

An impromptu press conference held after two union organizers were beaten up as they tried to enter the struck plant.

A packing house truck goes by a union picket.

13

A Modern Slave Trade

More than half the poor people who enter the United States illegally to seek work are from Hispanic nations. They come with hope, but because they work in the underground labor market they live in fear—victims of hunger, disease, extortion, and an exploitation often close to slavery.

Hunger for cheap labor has always found its way around the law. The African slave trade was banned after 1807, but slaves were smuggled into the United States for another fifty years; only the Civil War ended the illegal trade. As the American economy expanded, millions of men and women were needed to do the work of plowing, planting, and harvesting, of weaving, mining, and building. The poor, the hungry, and the homeless were drawn from every corner of the globe to fill jobs in America.

Many immigrants came under contract. But soon more

workers were being brought in than there were jobs to fill. The result: wages were pushed even lower. Trade union pressure upon Congress led to a law banning employers from contracting for labor in foreign lands.

But again, the hunger for profits found its way around the law. As soon as immigrants arrived, labor contractors took them in tow, hustling them directly from ship to work gang, promising them good wages. At mine or mill or railroad construction camp, a work boss took over from the contractor, hiring his gang out to the employer. Strangers in a new land, unable to speak English, the workers were packed into shacks, forced to buy supplies at high prices in company stores, and paid wages much lower than they had been promised. They were trapped, the victims of a new kind of slave trade.

Whenever America fell into a depression, unemployed workers blamed their troubles on "the foreigners." Then more laws went on the books, making it harder for people to enter the country or become citizens. In 1882, when Congress passed a law barring all Chinese immigrants, some employers began importing Japanese labor. And corporations running the huge West Coast farms turned south for other hands to do the work at cheap prices. Out of Mexico the needed workers came, to enter as aliens a land their nation had once owned.

It was a new law that forced the Mexicans into illegal entry. In 1917, Congress decreed that immigrants had to be able to read and write—a standard many Mexicans could not meet. Yet employers wanted cheap Mexican labor, so, as we saw in Chapter 8, the gates were opened for some years through the bracero program. When it ended in

1964, business found a way to get around the law. Employers who wanted cheap labor turned to traders who could supply it.

Here is how the traffic in illegal aliens works. Smugglers—called "coyotes"—sneak workers across the border from Mexico. Contractors on the U.S. side provide the migrants with jobs. Smuggler and contractor work in close harmony. The deals they make satisfy the demands of farmers, ranchers, railroads, mining companies, and everyone else who profits by cheap labor.

It costs money to be smuggled across the border, and even those who pay may not always make it into the United States. Chances of capture are much higher than in the past. Today, all sorts of computerized detection devices placed along the border will alert the U.S. Border Patrol if someone passes near them. Helicopters and light planes with powerful spotlights watch overhead. Migrants who hope to get through the technological barriers and the force of 2,000 Border Patrol officers have to pay many people: the person who arranges the trip, the guide who sees the migrants across the border, the driver who picks up the aliens and takes them inland.

There are only two ways to cross the boundary illegally—by walking or swimming. Several hundred people a year drown trying to cross the Rio Grande or the other water barrier, the All American Canal. (The canal runs near the border from Calexico, California, to Yuma, Arizona.) If a worker does not die in the water, he risks death in the desert. When there is danger ahead, smugglers will desert their cargo.

A group of El Salvadoreans was smuggled in from Mexico in July 1980. Thirty of them, lost in the Arizona desert, ran out of water. Thirteen died of dehydration. A twenty-two-year-old, convicted of smuggling them, faced a maximum penalty of five years in prison and a $2,000 fine. People who try to come across the border from Mexico are not the only ones who may die in the attempt. Late in 1980, twenty-two Dominicans who tried to slip into the United States aboard a freighter—they paid $3,000 each to the smuggler—died of asphyxiation because they were packed so tightly into the ship's ballast tank.

The world's poor have always wanted to enter the United States. Over a million illegal aliens were caught by the U.S. Immigration and Naturalization Service in each of the last three years of the 1970s. About half that many immigrants were admitted legally in that period. Mexico is the biggest source of illegal immigrants; about half a million come each year. (This flow is two-way. Over 40 percent of them go back to Mexico.) Others come from all over Latin America, from Canada, Europe, Asia, the islands of the Pacific, the Middle East—every part of the world. They arrive by ship and plane from their native lands, crossing borders north and south of the U.S.

Estimates of the number of illegal aliens who live in the United States vary a lot. There is no way to get an accurate count, because illegal aliens naturally don't want to expose themselves. If caught, they are confined, then evicted. The estimates run from three million to twelve million; experts think that 60 percent of these people are Mexicans.

About 10 or 15 percent of the illegal aliens now living

here entered the United States legally. That is, they came as temporary visitors—tourists or foreign students. But they violated the terms of their admission by overstaying their time or by taking jobs.

The tough immigration laws foster a modern "slave" trade and big profits for the international smugglers who run it. The traders in illegal aliens have created a vast network to handle their business. They have offices around the country, ready to supply employers with however many workers they need. It is a multimillion-dollar business, and there is no end to the brutal way smugglers and labor contractors treat their human cargoes. The smugglers are quick to develop new routes and methods as the INS or the police of foreign nations discover their old ones.

The great majority of illegal aliens live and work in three states—California, Texas, and Florida—and in two cities—New York and Chicago. But some also work at jobs almost everywhere else in the country. Sasha Lewis, a leading investigator of the illegal trade in immigrants, reports that:

They work not only in the fields of California, Texas, Florida, and Arizona, but at farming Christmas trees in Washington and Oregon, rolling irrigation pipes in Idaho, roping cattle and mending fences and driving tractors in Wyoming, bringing in the harvest of grain in Kansas, Colorado, Nebraska, and Missouri—an estimated 64,000 work in the grain belt alone.

They work in the light industries strung out along Interstate 80 near Chicago, in restaurants where the politically powerful dine in Washington, D.C., as domestics in New Jersey, at every kind of job in the San Francisco Bay Area, and they make up an estimated three-quarters of the minority work force in Boston's metropolitan region. They harvest every American crop from avocados to tobacco. They clean the dirty laundry of Nevada hotel–casino complexes. They sew in garment sweatshops in Los Angeles and New York. There is no end to the work they do nor the places they do it, for America still hungers for cheap labor, labor that is docile, labor that will remain muffled when the hours are long and the paychecks short.

Many thousands of illegal immigrants find themselves living in what amounts to slavery. The law calls it "involuntary servitude." It occurs whenever a worker is forced, by whatever means, to stay at a job he does not want. If he is forced to work off a debt to his boss, his employer is guilty of "peonage." The size of the debt doesn't matter. It makes no difference whether the worker agreed to take the job in the first place. Nor does the boss have to hold the worker in chains or under lock and key. The threat of force is enough to make it slavery. Employers simply take advantage of the risky position of illegal immigrants.

The laws against peonage go back to the time right after the Civil War, when freed slaves were often forced to work by their former masters. Tenant farmers and sharecroppers who got into debt were made to work out what they owed. The practice of peonage has continued to the present day. This is what happens:

• Ana Beatrix, a Guatemalan woman, was brought to work in a Maryland family as a maid. She was paid under twenty cents an hour. She was ordered never to leave the house, and was forbidden to talk to anyone outside the family. She was not given the room she had been promised, but was made to sleep in a dark, damp basement corner. After a year she found the courage to escape and tell her story.

• In Bartow, Florida, two Mexican girls, aged twelve and fifteen, were held prisoner by a labor contractor who hired them out as field workers to farmers. Federal agents rescued the girls.

• In the Texas Panhandle, workers were locked up every night in a barn by a sugar beet farmer.

• In Arkansas, Durward Woosley, a smuggler of aliens, sold Mexican immigrants to farmers for $400 each. The farmers held back each Mexican's wages until the $400 was worked off, and then sold the aliens to other farmers for $400. The Mexican workers never got any cash— in essence, each farmer was getting free labor. Some Mexicans were forced to work for three or four farmers in a row and never made a penny the whole time they were in the United States. Woosley, who pleaded guilty after he was arrested, had paid recruiters $30 a head to bring Mexicans over the border. He sold over 5,000 workers for $400 a piece, or more, before being caught.

• In Truxno, Louisiana, Connie Ray Alford, a chicken farmer, pleaded guilty to chaining up two of his workers in a chicken coop to keep them from running away. The victims were Isaul and Fidel Mata, Mexican illegals; they and nine other Mexicans were held captive for four months, threatened with guns, and forced to work twelve hours a day, seven days a week, for substandard wages.

• In southern Arizona, fifteen-year-old Rosa was a live-in servant for the household of an executive. The executive had arranged for her to be smuggled in across the border. She was not allowed outdoors except to attend church. One day she was raped by the executive and became pregnant. The man paid for the delivery, forced her to put the baby up for adoption, and then said she would have to work for him for nothing to pay back the medical expenses. A social worker rescued Rosa, but she refused to press charges out of fear for her life.

There is not as much peonage in the Southwest, because it is so close to the Mexican border and is flooded with illegal alien workers. But where there is a shortage of farm labor—in the citrus and winter vegetable belts of Florida, in the potato fields of Idaho, on the tobacco farms of Virginia and North Carolina—peonage is not uncommon.

Living conditions for illegal aliens are often terrible. Farm workers have been supplied with plastic sheets in place of tents and blankets, or left to shelter in packing crates or abandoned cars. Landlords bleed their tenants: in Texas, forty-five men were found crammed into three bedrooms, and each was paying $20 a week in rent! In San Diego, eighty-three people were reportedly living in one two-bedroom house.

Even if a boss is not brutal to his workers and pays them the minimum wage or better, other people may take advantage of them. Sasha Lewis reports:

Landlords collect a month's rent in advance, and after a week or so call in the INS to deport the tenants, then fill the building again with a new group of renters, collecting four months' rent for every month of housing given. Runners bring food to those in hiding at twice or three times its cost. Gangs wait to rob the worker of his or her pay on payday, beating and raping in added viciousness. Racketeers posing as lawyers promise to get legal work permits, collecting their payments in advance and delivering nothing. Forgers sell fake documents [needed for identification] on the installment plan for $1,000 a set—yet the documents are not good enough to pass inspection.

In recent years, with millions of American workers unemployed, this question has been posed: Do alien workers fill a need, or do they crowd the job field?

Hispanic leaders say aliens are needed—that they do the menial jobs Americans don't want, that the crops couldn't be harvested without them. And they actually increase tax revenues by paying for Social Security services they seldom use.

Dr. Vernon Briggs, a labor economist at Cornell University, has studied illegal immigration for over fifteen years. His research shows that illegal aliens do compete with Americans for jobs in all fields where they work. At the same time, they push wages down and slow moves toward unionization or improvement of working conditions. He and others claim there is no shortage of Americans competing for the jobs aliens seek. Blacks in Miami said the same when tens of thousands of Cubans flooded in during the spring of 1980. The blacks, already suffering from heavy unemployment, feared that Cubans would be given jobs ahead of them.

What to do about it? Some propose that border patrols be tightened. In Congress, bills have been introduced that would allow the government to fine employers who knowingly hire illegal aliens. Hispanic leaders say such penalties would lead employers to discriminate against *all* Hispanics. Americans concerned for civil liberties fear that attempts to control illegal immigration may lead to laws requiring all workers—citizens and aliens alike—to carry identification cards. Such laws, they say, would mean that every American citizen would come under tighter government control.

The problem of what to do about illegal aliens torments the Congress and the courts. Facts enough to make the problem clear have been gathered after thorough study by commissions. But there is no easy solution. Neither conservatives nor liberals agree among themselves on what policy should be. Public opinion polls show the country at large shifts in its view of the emotional issue. So long as we avoid coming to grips with the problem, the misery of the millions who live and work in the underground labor market will continue.

14

Struggle for Justice

Listen to the voice of Cesar Chavez:

Our strikers here in Delano [California] have been under the gun, they have been kicked and beaten and herded by dogs, they have been cursed and ridiculed, they have been stripped and chained and jailed, they have been sprayed with the poisons used in the vineyards.

But they have been taught not to lie down and die nor to flee in shame, but to resist with every ounce of human endurance and spirit. To resist not with retaliation in kind, but to overcome with love and compassion, with ingenuity and creativity, with hard work and longer hours, with stamina and patient tenacity, with truth and public appeal, with friends and allies, with mobility and discipline, with politics and law, and with prayer and fasting.

They were not trained in a month or even a year; after all, this new harvest season will mark our fourth full year of strike and even now we continue to plan and prepare for the years to come.

*Time accomplishes for the poor what money does for the rich.
. . . God knows that we are not beasts of burden, agricultural
implements, or rented slaves; we are men.*

*We are men locked in a death struggle against man's inhumanity
to man. And this struggle itself gives meaning to our life and ennobles
our dying.*

Delano was where, in 1965, La Huelga, the grape strike,
began. Under the leadership of Cesar Chavez, the strike
unified field workers of all ethnic groups. The longest agricultural strike in history, it ended in victory in 1970.
Against great odds, the workers won higher wages and
improved working conditions.

When the protest erupted in the 1960s, the newspapers
said, "At last the sleeping Mexican has awakened!" At last?
That was nonsense. The Hispanics have a rich history of
resistance to oppression. It began long before the 1960s.
When Chavez organized the Chicano farm workers in California, he was carrying on a great tradition of struggle
against exploitation and discrimination. The Puerto Ricans, the Cubans, the Mexicans—all fought for freedom
from Spanish rule. When robbed of their land or their
rights, they always resisted the oppressor.

For years after the United States took from them a huge
piece of their territory in the 1840s, Chicanos led by such
men as Juan Cortina carried on guerrilla warfare against
the occupiers of their land. Some Chicanos rebelled against
oppression by taking to the highway: they became *bandidos,*
stealing to survive. Anglos called men like Tiburcio Vasquez criminals, but Vasquez was moved by the spirit of
revenge. White settlers in California were treating Chica-

nos like dogs. Vasquez, Juan Flores, Joaquín Murieta—they fought back against the tyranny of the Anglos. They were hunted down as bandits, but poor Chicanos in the hills supported and shielded them. The bandits were doing what these hungry, downtrodden people wished *they* could do.

A more organized form of resistance came into being when Chicano workers began to form labor unions. Mexican Americans led strikes in the Texas Panhandle in 1883. In the 1890s and early 1900s, La Alianza Hispanoamericana organized workers on the railroads and in the copper mines of Arizona. There were strikes, often broken by armed deputy sheriffs, often ending with union leaders sentenced to prison. Some labor leaders believed that organizing field workers was almost impossible, because migrants were unskilled and could easily be replaced if they tried to strike. But as early as 1903, Chicanos organized and struck in the sugar beet fields of Colorado. Other workers struck the Los Angeles streetcar line, and in Florida cigar makers walked off the job. Their militancy was fired by reports of revolutionary movements in Cuba and Mexico.

The Great Depression heated up the struggle. Powerful farmers tried to make up their losses by pushing the wages of migrant workers even lower. When the migrants tried to organize, the growers declared war. They used the Immigration and Naturalization Service to deport Mexican union leaders; they got relief agencies to deny help to workers; they got sheriffs to terrorize the strikers, the courts to jail them, and vigilantes to kill them. Nevertheless, the great labor upheaval in California won the support of thousands of Mexicans. One of the most extensive farm strikes in American history took place in 1933, when 12,000 migrant cotton pickers—80 percent of them Mexican— walked out of the fields in the San Joaquin Valley.

Chicano factory workers also organized in the 1930s. By then, women were part of the stream of workers moving north from Mexico. The migrants were still mostly single men, but a growing number of families and even single women were coming to the United States. Women were wanted in the clothing and food processing industries— bosses believed they could exploit women even more than men. Thousands entered the garment sweatshops of the Southwest. And they, too, joined unions, trying to raise wages that fell as low as fifty cents a week. In steel, packing, longshore, furniture—wherever they found jobs—Chicanos helped to build the unions.

By 1945, Chicano workers were rooted in the U.S. labor movement. Many fewer of them worked on the farms; the majority of Chicanos now lived in the cities. Yet it was La Huelga—the militant struggle of farm workers in California, led by Cesar Chavez—that woke the whole nation to the oppression of Chicanos.

Chavez proved to be a master of modern communications. He was able to win public support for his strikers by such dramatic actions as calling for a national boycott of grapes. He was able to build alliances with other groups. He was able to unite Anglo and Chicano college students with uneducated farm workers in the common cause. He broke down the old barrier between poor Chicanos and middle-class Mexican Americans.

La Huelga became more than a struggle for higher wages and better working conditions. It was a movement of the poor for deep social change, a force for ending racism and inequality.

Militant leaders like Chavez, Reies López Tijerina, and Rodolfo ("Corky") Gonzales also captured national attention for the problems and goals of Chicanos in the 1960s. Gonzales, a worker in the Colorado sugar beet fields at ten, a featherweight boxer and poet, founded La Cruzada para la Justicia. A family organization, it ran a school, a bookstore, and a social center, and published a newspaper. It demonstrated against police brutality and supported mass actions against the Vietnam war. Gonzales campaigned for Chicano studies in schools and colleges. Marching and picketing, Mexican-Americans demanded equal justice, more jobs, a fair share in federal poverty programs. "Power is respected in this society," Gonzales said. "We need brown power to offset Anglo power."

Tijerina was born on a cotton sack in a Texas field his mother was hoeing. A migrant worker in childhood, he became a preacher and set out to help his people get back their land—land granted to Mexicans by Spain and then the Republic of Mexico. As we have seen, the Treaty of Guadalupe Hidalgo bound the United States to protect the land holdings of Mexicans in the American Southwest, but the land was soon appropriated by Anglos. Tijerina felt that Chicanos had a just claim to this land, which had been taken, he said, by fraud—fraud the U.S. government had had a part in. He believed that if Chicanos could force the courts to listen to their just claims, they would win back their land and put an end to their poverty.

Tijerina built up the Alianza Federal de Mercedes, or Federal Alliance of Land Grants. In 1967, he and three hundred and fifty Alianza members occupied Carson National Forest in New Mexico, claiming 1,400 acres as *ejido*—that is, communal or village land. (According to Hispano-Mexican law, *ejido* could not be sold and was to be held in common by the people.) Tijerina and his followers were finally forced to leave, but the national news of their extraordinary action taught many Americans something about the way Hispanics in the Southwest have been treated.

Later, Tijerina's group made a spectacular raid on a courthouse in New Mexico to attract attention to his cause; the action won wide sympathy, especially among youth. By 1970, several organizations of young Chicanos had formed, all proposing to change a society they found to be unjust, and to win a life of dignity.

United actions against discrimination have been taken by Hispanics in many arenas. Cases are brought in the courts against segregated schools and swimming pools. Campaigns are waged for a fair share of education grants and public housing, for more jobs and job-training programs. Hispanics demand a chance to help make decisions affecting their own lives; they demand appointments in the public agencies that administer social and economic programs. Meeting human needs is the basic job of such American institutions, but their response to the needs of ethnic minorities, says Professor Joan W. Moore, "has been

poor. It continues to be poor. Sometimes it is utterly de-
structive." Moore, who is an expert in the field of Mexican
American studies, adds that important changes have been
made in the last few decades, but far more needs to be
done.

The Puerto Ricans, too, have built dozens of organizations devoted to advancing their interests on the mainland.
A number of these are based in New York City. New York's
one million Puerto Ricans make it the largest Puerto Rican
city in the world. The one million are mainly poor working
people. Without them, hotels, restaurants, hospitals, the
garment industry, and many small factories and shops
would collapse. They share the problems of their brothers
and sisters in scores of other American cities.

The Puerto Rican Forum dates back to the 1950s, when
young Puerto Ricans felt the need for a community-wide
organization in New York. The Forum first focused on
youth and educational advance. Out of its work came Aspira and the Puerto Rican Community Development Project. Aspira is nationally known for guiding and
encouraging Puerto Ricans as they seek higher education
and professional training. The Development Project runs
a broader program aimed at promoting a sense of ethnic
identity and building community strength.

The Puerto Rican Family Institute, an agency started by
Puerto Rican social workers in New York, helps to provide
services to families who have just immigrated. Other groups
run self-help centers, maintain athletic programs, and support Puerto Rican literature, music, theater, and art.

A different, more militant Puerto Rican organization was

the Young Lords. One such group, now disbanded, started as a street gang in Chicago in 1969. Puerto Rican young people turned their backs on the cautious ways of their elders and borrowed ideas from the radical Black Panthers. They took over a seminary and demanded that it do more for the poor on the Near North Side of Chicago. Then they occupied a church and opened a day-care center in its basement. They seized urban renewal land and turned it into a People's Park (developers had planned to build a tennis club on the site). The Young Lords had to act on behalf of the poor, they said, because the city of Chicago was doing nothing to meet their needs.

In the early 1970s, another Young Lords group started up, this one in New York. These Young Lords took over a church in East Harlem and started a free children's break-fast program. They "borrowed" a mobile clinic to give slum children free examinations for tuberculosis. They took militant actions to improve hospital care in East Har-lem and the Bronx.

The Young Lords were not the educated middle-class Puerto Ricans who usually provided leadership. They were mostly the children of poor workers, raised in the barrio. But they spoke English—they could tell the Anglos what they wanted.

What about political action on a broader scale? Judging by their numbers alone, Hispanics should be holding politi-cal office almost everywhere in the country. In the South-west, for instance, state legislatures would be 10 to 20 percent Hispanic if the Hispanic population were fairly represented. But Hispanics actually hold less than 1 percent of the seats in the legislatures of Southwestern states. And even in recent times there have never been more than a few Hispanic congressmen, senators, or governors. California has a huge Chicano population, but just ten years ago, not one Chicano sat in the California legislature. New York City's one million Puerto Ricans have rarely been able to elect a Puerto Rican candidate. In 1970, Herman Badillo of New York became the first Puerto Rican congressman. Very few Hispanics have followed him to Washington; very few are in state legislatures or on city councils.

Why so few? There are several reasons. Hispanics are very much a young population, with many below voting age. Even when young people reach the age to vote, a sadly small number choose to do so—Hispanic *or* Anglo. The Hispanics are also a mostly poor people, with far less education, on the average, than Anglos. Such citizens tend not to register or vote. In the United States, it is older, better educated people with good incomes who turn out to vote in the largest numbers.

The response of individual Hispanics to discrimination and injustice follows historical patterns. Some decide that they want to assimilate into American society, to become completely a part of it. Usually these are the educated and the prosperous, who can use their skills to find good places within society. Paul, who has moved toward assimilation, puts it this way:

I don't want to be known as a Mexican American, but only as an American. I was born in this country and raised among Ameri-

cans. I think like an Anglo, I talk like one, and I dress like one. It's true I don't look like an Anglo and sometimes I am rejected by them, but it would be worse if I spoke Spanish or said that I was of Mexican descent. I am sorry I do not get along well with my parents, but their views are old-fashioned. They still see themselves as Mexican, and they do not understand me. Often we have arguments, but I ignore them. In fact, I had to move away from my home because of our disagreements. I wish those people who are always making noise about being Mexican-Americans would be quiet. We would all be better off if they would accept things as they are. I just want a good education. I don't want to be poor. I don't want to be discriminated against.

At the other extreme are those who proudly assert their ethnic heritage. They proclaim their nationalism. They think that to assimilate is impossible and not even desirable. Roberto had this to say:

I am proud of being a Mexican American. We have a rich heritage. Mexico is a great country that is progressing fast. It has a wonderful history and culture. My family is the most important thing in the world for me. I owe my parents everything. . . . I don't want to be like the "Paddys," [Anglos] because they don't care about their families; they just care about themselves and making money. They don't like anybody who is different. At school, the teachers ignored you if they knew you weren't going to college, and most of us Mexicans couldn't afford to go. The things I learned at school were against what my parents had taught me. I had to choose my parents, because they are old and they need my help and understanding. Most people, even some Mexican Americans, look down on us because we are Mexicans, and I hate them. It is unhealthy and unnatural to want to be something you are not.

Some criticize Hispanics like Paul for trying to make it, leaving others in their group at the bottom of the heap. It would be better to work for revolutionary change in the system, they say; that would end economic exploitation and wipe out racism and discrimination.

The big majority are in the middle, like Rosa, a teen-ager who has shaped her identity within both cultures. She says:

I am happy to be an American of Mexican descent. Because I am a Mexican, I learned to be close to my family, and they have been a source of strength and support for me. If things ever get too bad on the outside I could always come to them for comfort and understanding. My Spanish also helped me a lot in my education and will open a lot of doors for me when I look for a job. As an American I am happy to live in a great progressive country where we have the freedom to achieve anything we want. I feel all that I have achieved I owe to the help of my parents, the encouragement of my teachers, and the chance to live in this country. I feel very rich and fortunate because I have two cultures rather than just one.

People like Rosa value their ethnic tradition, prize their cultural differences. They want their uniqueness to be rec-ognized and accepted by the dominant Anglo society; they do not want to give it up. But they work for concessions from society, not for its overthrow. They seek changes that would make it serve human needs better.

Of course, no Hispanic is fixed in any position. Some who have assimilated change their minds, and join militant anti-assimilation groups; the opposite may happen as well. Others drift, taking one position today, another tomorrow, while still others are genuinely torn, feeling they would like the advantages of assimilation but would hate themselves if they rejected their Hispanic heritage.

But let's not forget discrimination. It is the basic problem. It is why most Hispanics remain poor and ill-educated in the first place. And it is why they find it hard to act for their own good. Fear and isolation make many say, "What's the use? What difference will political action make?" If Hispanics do decide politics is worthwhile, they find that society sometimes makes it hard for them even to vote. Anglo politicans have used fraud and intimidation at the polls. Literacy tests are a barrier, and so are laws that require voters to live in one area for a long period of time. Hispanics move a lot—back and forth to Puerto Rico, to Mexico. Voting districts are often gerrymandered—areas with sizable Hispanic populations are cut up into several voting districts so that Hispanics can't vote effectively as a bloc.

All this explains why no American minority has a smaller voice in politics than the Hispanics. But the picture is changing. Hispanics have formed organizations to encourage political action and to educate their people to its importance. La Causa, the goal of self-determination and self-respect, may be won only if Hispanic people mobilize to play their part in American political life. Without a voice in politics, you have no say in your own future.

Wherever laws are written, judicial decisions made, and executive reforms shaped, pressure must be applied to assure any minority's full rights. When alliances can be formed with other ethnic or racial groups, the chance of success is so much the better.

Forming such an alliance is not an easy thing to do. While minority organizations have things in common, they also have differences in policy and methods. Organizations have all the weaknesses of the human beings they are made up of. To overcome differences for the sake of the common good is hard to do. But how to achieve justice and equality without unity?

A Chicano leader in Texas showed recently that finding paths to unity can bring victory. In 1981, Henry Gabriel Cisneros ran for mayor of San Antonio, the nation's ninth largest city, and won by an impressive majority—62 percent of the vote. The thirty-three-year-old teacher and political leader buried his Anglo opponent in an avalanche of votes from every part of the city. Cisneros became the first Mexican American mayor of San Antonio since 1842, when Texas was still an independent republic. He is now the first Hispanic mayor of any of the nation's ten largest cities.

Earlier, during his three terms as city councilman, Cisneros worked hard to build bridges between the Chicanos, who are 53 percent of the population, and non-Hispanics. Now, he says, the coalition of Chicanos, blacks, and whites "can be put to work for San Antonio."

For most of us this story of the Hispanic Americans has been neglected or hidden. Yet that history, that life in the past, has shaped our present, no matter what ethnic group we ourselves may belong to. Not to know that past is to be blind to the realities of today. If we are out of touch with what has happened to a people so central to American life, then we cannot know where we are now, and where we may be heading.

Bibliography

This is not an exhaustive list of the research material I used in preparing this book. It does not contain references to those valuable sources, the files of contemporary newspapers and journals. I owe special thanks to the New York Times *for its coverage of Hispanic news, in particular to its reporters David Vidal and John M. Crewdson; and to the journals* Agenda *and* Aztlan. *Nelida Perez, librarian of the Center for Puerto Rican Studies, John Jay College, New York, was generous with her time and knowledge, and so was Victoria Ortiz, whose personal library on Hispanic affairs was made available to me.*

A number of the titles listed below are now in paperback.

Acuna, Rodolfo. *Occupied America: A History of Chicanos.* 2d ed. New York: Harper & Row, 1981.

Alford, Harold J. *The Proud Peoples: Heritage and Culture of Spanish-Speaking Peoples in the United States.* New York: David McKay Co., 1972.

Appel, John and Selma. *The Distorted Image: Stereotype and Caricature in American Popular Graphics, 1850–1922.* New York: Anti-Defamation League, n.d.

Barrera, Mario. *Race and Class in the Southwest.* Notre Dame, Ind.: University of Notre Dame Press, 1979.

Briggs, Vernon M. *The Chicano Worker.* Austin: University of Texas Press, 1977.

Camarillo, Albert. *Chicanos in a Changing Society.* Cambridge, Mass.: Harvard University Press, 1979.

Council on Interracial Books for Children. *Stereotypes, Distortions, and Omissions in U.S. History Textbooks.* New York: Council on Interracial Books for Children, 1977.

Dinnerstein, Leonard, and Reimers, David M. *Ethnic Americans: A History of Immigration and Assimilation.* New York: Harper & Row, 1975.

Ehrlich, Paul R. *The Golden Door: International Migration, Mexico and the United States.* New York: Ballantine Books, 1979.

Farb, Peter. *Humankind.* Boston: Houghton Mifflin Co., 1978.

Fernandez, Raul A. *The U.S.–Mexico Border.* Notre Dame, Ind.: University of Notre Dame Press, 1977.

Fitzpatrick, Joseph P. *Puerto Rican Americans: The Meaning of Migration to the Mainland.* Englewood Cliffs, N.J.: Prentice-Hall, 1971.

Forbes, Jack D. *The Indian in America's Past.* Englewood Cliffs, N.J.: Prentice-Hall, 1964.

Galarza, Ernesto. *Barrio Boy.* Notre Dame, Ind.: University of Notre Dame Press, 1971.

Gibson, Charles. *Spain in America.* New York: Harper & Row, 1966.

Gomez, David F. *Somos Chicanos: Strangers in Our Own Land.* Boston: Beacon Press, 1973.

Greer, Colin, ed. *Divided Society: The Ethnic Experience in America.* New York: Basic Books, 1974.

Horgan, Paul. *Conquistadores in North America.* New York: Macmillan Co., 1963.

Lewis, Gordon K. *Puerto Rico: Freedom and Power in the Caribbean.* New York: Monthly Review Press, 1963.

Lewis, Sasha G. *Slave Trade Today: American Exploitation of Illegal Aliens.* Boston: Beacon Press, 1979.

Lopez, Alfredo. *The Puerto Rican Papers: Notes on the Reemergence of a Nation.* Indianapolis: Bobbs-Merrill Co., 1973.

Maldonado-Denis, Manuel. *Puerto Rico: A Socio-Historic Interpretation.* New York: Vintage Books, 1972.

McWilliams, Carey. *North from Mexico.* Philadelphia: J. B. Lippincott Co., 1949.

Meltzer, Milton. *Bound for the Rio Grande: The Mexican Struggle, 1845–1850.* New York: Alfred A. Knopf, 1974.

Mindel, Charles H., and Habenstein, Robert W. *Ethnic Families in America: Patterns and Variations.* New York: Elsevier, 1976.

Moore, Joan W. *Mexican Americans.* Englewood Cliffs, N.J.: Prentice-Hall, 1970.

Pendle, George. *A History of Latin America.* New York: Penguin Books, 1980.

Pietri, Pedro. *Puerto Rican Obituary.* New York: Monthly Review Press, 1973.

Pifer, Alan. *Bilingual Education and the Hispanic Challenge.* New York: Carnegie Corporation of New York, 1979.

Simmen, Edward, ed. *Pain and Promise: The Chicano Today.* New York: New American Library, 1972.

Steiner, Stan. *La Raza.* New York: Harper & Row, 1970.

Stoddard, Ellwyn R. *Mexican Americans.* New York: Random House, 1973.

Vega, Bernardo. *Memoirs of Bernardo Vega.* New York: Monthly Review Press, in press.

Wagenheim, Kal, with Olga Jiminez de Wagenheim. *The Puerto Ricans.* New York: Anchor Books, 1973.

Wakefield, Dan. *Island in the City.* Boston: Houghton Mifflin Co., 1959.

Wilson Quarterly. "Puerto Rico." Spring, 1980:119–50.

Index

Africans, 11, 49, 92, 93, 95, 117
Alianza Hispanoamericana, 129
Anglos, 75–77, 85, 86, 93–95, 99, 105, 131, 135–36
Argentinians, 17
Aspira, 133
assimilation, 135–38
automation, 20
Aztecs, 71–72

Badillo, Herman, 135
Balboa, Vasco Nunez de, 8
barrios, 16–25, 61–68, 96, 134
Bay of Pigs invasion, 53
Betances, Ramon E., 28
bilingual programs, 55, 107–11
birth control, 30

blacks, in Cuba, 49; in Puerto Rico, 26–27; in Miami, 53, 126
bodegas, 17, 24
bracero program, 82–83, 118
Briggs, Vernon, 125

Cabeza de Vaca, Nuñez, 8–9
California, 8, 9, 61–68, 77–78, 121
Castro, Fidel, 44, 49, 51–52, 53, 54
Catholicism, 12–13, 94
Chavez, Cesar, 83, 112, 127–28, 130–31
Chicanos, 1–6, 61–88, 100–104, 112–16, 127–33, 136–37
Chinese Americans, 93, 118

Chinese Exclusion Act, 93, 118
Cisneros, Henry Gabriel, 139
civil rights laws, 98
Colombians, 14, 16
Columbus, Christopher, 7–8, 10, 47
Coronado, Francisco Vásquez de, 9
Cortez, Hernando, 71
Cortina, Juan, 128
Creoles (criollos), 27, 49, 72
Crusade for Justice (Cruzada para la Justicia), 131
Cuba, 9, 27, 28: Castro revolution in, 51; economy of, 49–51; history of, 49–51; independence movement in, 49–51; migration from, 44–47, 53–59; missile crisis, 53
Cubans, 17, 44–60: aid to, 54, 57; education of, 54, 103; in Miami, 53–60; middle class among, 47, 54; political refugees, 47; poverty among, 88; protest by, 128

De León family, 44–47
De Soto, Hernando, 9
Delano, 127–38
discrimination, 88, 89–99, 103, 126, 132, 138
Dominican Republic, 8, 37
Dominicans, 14, 17, 37–43, 120

Ecuadorians, 14, 17
education, 54, 100–111, 132

Federal Alliance of Land Grants, 132
Flores, Juan, 129
Florida, 8, 9, 44–47, 54, 121

Galarza, Ernesto, 61–68, 101–2
Garay, Bernabé, 2–3
genetic mixture, 10–11, 95
Gold Rush of 1849, 77
Gonzales, Rodolfo "Corky," 81, 131
Gonzalez, Augustin, 111
Gonzalez, Silvia, 60
Grant, Ulysses S., 74
grape strike, 112, 127–28
Great Depression, 80–81, 129
Greer, Colin, 110

Halsell, Grace, 85–86
health, 29, 33, 88, 117
Hidalgo, Miguel, 73
Hispanic, defined, 12
Hitler, Adolf, 93
Holocaust, 93
housing, 22, 30, 45, 62–63, 66, 84, 87–88, 124–25

illegal aliens, 3, 70, 117–26
immigration laws, 79, 93, 118–19, 121, 126
immigration: Cuban, 44–47, 53–60; Hispanic, 1–5;

illegal, 2–3, 117–26; laws on, 79, 93, 118–19, 126; Mexican, 1–3, 61–68, 79–83; Puerto Rican, 32–36
identity, Hispanic, 10–15, 35
incomes, 3, 31, 47, 70–71, 80–81, 86–87
Indians; *see* Native Americans
intermarriage, 11
Irish, 16, 94

Japanese Americans, 93, 118
Jefferson, Thomas, 78
Jews, 16, 93

La Huelga, 128, 130–31
labor unions, 22, 36, 83, 95, 112–16, 118, 127–31
land reform, 30
Lau vs. Nichols, 110
Lewis, Sasha, 121

Martí, José, 50
mestizos, 72
Mexican Americans, 1–6, 61–88, 100–104, 112–16, 127–33, 136–37
Mexican Revolution, 80
Mexican War, 73–74, 105
Mexico, 1–2, 105; history of, 71–83
Miami, 45–47, 53–60
migrant labor, 1–3, 61–68, 83–86
migration, Puerto Ricans, 32–36

Montezuma, 71
Moore, Joan W., 133
Morales Carrion, Arturo, 11–12
Muñoz Marín, Luis, 30
Murieta, Joaquín, 129

nationalism, 26, 29, 136–37
Native Americans, 7, 8, 9, 11, 49, 69, 71, 72, 78, 92, 93, 95
Nazis, 93
New Mexico, 9, 69

"Operation Bootstrap," 30–31
Ortiz family, 33–36

peonage, 122–24
Pietri, Pedro, 20
plantation system, 11
Platt Amendment, 50–51
pluralism, 137–38
police brutality, 98
political action, 134–35, 138–40
political refugees, 47
Polk, James, 74
Ponce de León, Juan, 8, 26
population: Cuban, in New York, 47, 57; in Miami, 47; in Los Angeles, 57; Dominican, in New York, 37; in Dominican Republic, 37; Hispanic, in Latin America, 3; in New York

City, 4, 16, 32; in Los
Angeles, 4; in Miami, 4; in
U.S., 6; Mexican American,
in U.S., 68, 69; Puerto
Rican, on mainland, 23;
in New York City, 32,
133
poverty, 2, 3, 23, 27, 56, 86–
88, 117
prejudice, 54, 93, 97
Puerto Rican Community
Development Project, 133
Puerto Rican Family
Institute, 133
Puerto Rican Forum, 133
Puerto Rico: economy of, 29–
32; history of, 26–36;
independence movement,
27; migration from, 32–
36; and "Operation
Bootstrap," 30–31; poverty
in, 29; unemployment in,
32; U.S. role in, 28–29; and
welfare, 32
Puerto Ricans, 11, 18–23, 26–
36, 88, 104, 105, 128, 133–
35

race, identity and, 10–13, 73
racism, 72, 75, 77–78, 88,
89–99: action against,
131–32; defined, 92;
institutionalized, 96; in the
media, 90; profits from, 96
ranching, 75–76
Roosevelt, Theodore, 29

Salvadoreans, 120
Scott, Winfield, 74
segregation, 77, 96, 103, 132
Seidman, Laurence, 75
slavery, 11, 49, 72–76, 117,
122
smugglers, 121
Soviet Union, 53, 56
Spanish American War, 28,
50
Spanish culture, 12, 14, 55,
105, 106, 136–38
Spanish Empire, influence of,
10–15
Spanish explorers and
conquistadors, 7–11, 22,
49, 71–72
Spanish Harlem, 18–19
Spanish language, 12–13, 35,
55, 105–11
Steinbeck, John, 90
stereotypes, 90–92, 105
sugar production, 27, 49, 50

teaching English as second
language, 108
Texas Rangers, 98
Texas Revolution, 73–74
Tijerina, Reies Lopez, 131
tourism, 31
Treaty of Guadalupe
Hidalgo, 74–75, 77, 131

underground labor market, 3,
117–26
undocumented residents,
117–26

United Farm Workers, 83,
112–16, 127–28
U.S. Commission on Civil
Rights, 98, 100
U.S. Border Patrol, 2, 80, 83,
98, 119, 126
U.S. Immigration and
Naturalization Service,
120, 121, 125, 129
U.S. Marine Corps, 50
U.S.–Mexican border region,
2, 70, 119

Vasquez, Tiburcio, 128
Vásquez de Ayllón, Lucas,
8
Vega, Bernardo, 21, 89–90
Vinas family, 37–43
voting, 138–40

women, 1, 4, 46, 72, 137
workers: cigar-making, 21;
cotton, 76–77; farm, 1, 3,
22–23, 66–67, 80, 83–86,
112–16, 124; garment, 33,
130; industry, 3, 62, 80,
130; mining, 77; railroads,
61, 64, 80; ranch, 3, 75–
76; service trades, 3, 21,
33, 62; stores, 15, 64;
undocumented, 117–26;
white collar, 23
World War I, 106–7
World War II, 30, 81, 83, 93,
97

Young Lords, 134

"Zoot Suit Riots," 97–98